JAY MCSWAIN

are YOU committed?

connecting God's people
to meaningful ministry

foreword by Dr. Jeff Iorg

Published in Atlanta, GA, by Jay McSwain

Scripture quotations are from the NEW INTERNATIONAL VERSION of the Bible. Copyright © 1990 Zondervan

McSwain, Jay
        Are You Committed? / Jay McSwain
        Includes bibliographical references
        ISBN 1-930856-59-8

                Printed in the United States of America

Contents

Acknowledgements

One of the hardest assignments in writing this book comes in acknowledging those who have contributed to my ability to be able to compile this book. There are so many that I will mention, but an equal number that will not make this list that still contributed to these insights.

First, let me thank the thousands of churches, that over the last ten years, have given our ministry insight in what it means to **connect** God's people into meaningful ministry. Hundreds of those churches have allowed me to get somewhat intimate into the dynamics of their churches as they relate to ministry involvement. Without your willingness to allow me to learn from you the insights I have gleaned, this book would have never been possible.

My spiritual father, Grady Roan, who is now in heaven and Don Moye, who mentored me through college, developed how I see the world from a biblical perspective and formed my spiritual character. Much of how I view God's people **connecting** in meaningful ministry was developed through their interaction with me, both formally and informally, in the beginning of my Christian life. These men continue to provide a compass for who and what I am today as a Christian. I will be forever grateful for their investment in my life.

Only God knows what would have become of my life if David Self, John Rushing and Norm Yukers had not seen past my fear of being involved in church. These men loved me, even when I gave little to nothing for their ministries at our church. They saw the potential I could have in impacting the Kingdom. My reengagement in ministry in 1995 came through them loving me where I was, but not allowing me to stay where I was. Gentlemen: thank-you for being obedient to God's call to get me out of the stands and onto the field to make a difference in the Kingdom. May your investment in me be **multiplied** many times over.

I consider Mark Hartman many things. Most notably, he is one of the wisest men in ministry I have ever known. Along with wisdom, Mark showed me how to have a balanced ministry with the five ministry objectives (worship, evangelism, discipleship, fellowship and ministry) receiving their due importance. Mark: thank-you for bringing me on staff at Council Road Baptist Church in 1998 to **connect** God's people to ministry. While on staff, you allowed me to glean from your balanced approach to ministry, along with your wisdom. When you moved to Sugarland, Texas to become the senior pastor at Sugar Creek Baptist Church, you continued to give me access to your wisdom and insight. You allowed me to see where I came up short at Council Road in putting together a holistic approach to **connecting** members to ministry. The genesis for this book came through your conversations with me on December 2nd and 3rd in 2003, while attending an advisory board meeting for my ministry. Your insights into our shortcomings at Council Road and that I have seen across the country, continue to challenge me to this day. As I have told you more than once, my nearly three years on your staff are three of the most fulfilling years of my life.

In addition to their technical skills in helping bring this book to fruition, I also thank my team for listening to me over the past several years flesh out most of this book, repeatedly interrupting them while they were working. Kraig Kelsey, Denise Mathias, Cecely Johnson, Missy Kelsey, Barbara Valerioti, Brendan Casey, Tim Wall and Sheila D'Amico—you are an incredible team! I count it a privilege to work alongside you. Thank-you for bringing your skills to bear, not only with this book, but in the many resources we are able to provide churches. Kraig: I especially thank-you for letting me hash out this book, sometimes in not so flattering ways, and then clean it up.

Without the generous financial and emotional support of my parents, my brother Keith and sister Sharon, there would have been no ministry to learn the insights that we have. Sharon: I will never forget my first year in seminary when you sent me $100 a month to help with my school expenses. You no more had the money to give me than I had to give you, but you sacrificed, and I will never forget—not to mention, all you have done for me in the years since.

My parents and brother: Your company, McCar Homes, has underwritten our ministry and thus allowed us to do what would only be a dream without your support. I will never be able to put into words my gratitude for your generosity. I hope that on the other side of heaven, you will know what your support has meant, not only to me and my ministry, but to the impact on the Kingdom.

Last and certainly not least, I thank my wife Ginger and my two beautiful daughters, Maggie and Mary. Ginger: you have allowed our bedroom to become a research library with books, computers and printers strung out over the room as I have written this book. You have listened to my thoughts about this book when I desired you to listen, and have left me alone when I needed solitude. I don't say it enough, but I am truly blessed to have you as a partner in life and in ministry. Maggie and Mary: thank-you for the times you brought me food and something to drink while I worked on this book. I pray that as you grow up, you will continue to have a desire to serve others in the name of Jesus.

You are all gifts. Thanks be to God from whom all blessings flow!

Foreword

by Dr. Jeff Iorg

President,
Golden Gate Baptist Theological Seminary

O ccasionally prophetic, always passionate, my friend Jay McSwain believes every church member should be an active minister in the kingdom of God. He has devoted his life to creating tools for churches to fulfill this mandate. Yet, this book is more than a tool. It is a definitive, holistic, systemic approach to solving the dilemma many church leaders face of how to lead their followers into ministry.

One of the key insights in this book is Jay's contention some church members should be trained for ministry outside the church, not as ministers in the church. It has been estimated, if every imaginable church ministry position were filled, only about 20% of Christians would be needed. What are the other 80% supposed to do? Serve in the community on behalf of the church! That insight alone is worth the price of the book.

This book takes on some of the assumptions many people make about what makes a church really successful. Rather than measure the number of cars in the parking lot or the people in the pews, Jay advocates clearly for a different measure of success – the number of believers actually involved in ministry. And, as he contends and illustrates, when large numbers of people are **equipped**, **encouraged**, **empowered**, and **multiplied** for ministry – church growth and kingdom growth will happen.

Many Christian leaders are concerned about the future of the church in North America and postulate various theories of what it will take to build a healthier future. This book is a sound biblical prescription, an antidote for short-term thinking or faddish pursuit of the latest program. Building believers into ministers and supporting them while they do their work is the recipe for long-term church health we all desire.

Dr. Jeff Iorg
President
Golden Gate Baptist Theological Seminary

Introduction

In 1995, I reengaged in ministry within my church. Some of the principles and concepts I highlight in this book were implemented unconsciously or unintentionally in my reengagement. However, many of the principles and concepts highlighted in the following pages were foreign to me, both on a conscious or unconscious level. Three years after reengaging, I was asked to help a growing church discover how to shut the back door through which members were exiting. This church staff position led to my creation of training, resources and tools for churches across the country and even in some foreign countries.

The creation of PLACE resources and training has taken me to literally hundreds of churches where I have trained staff and members on how to help members **identify** how God has created them for ministry. Also, I have led hundreds of training sessions on how to **connect** potential servants for ministries with ministry leaders. We assumed if we could move from self-discovery (helping members **identify** elements such as personality, spiritual gifts, abilities, passions and life experiences) to incorporating a process to **connect** members to ministry leaders that the church could claim "every member a minister." That was a WRONG assumption. WHY? We discovered it was not enough to be committed solely to an **identification** process, like PLACE Ministries (or any other), without also being committed to **other** key elements and principles at the same time.

Are You Committed? is a book to introduce the six elements that must be incorporated **simultaneously** for a church to have the potential to make "every member a minister." Without incorporating these six elements **simultaneously**, "every member a minister" will be a nice slogan without any possibility of ever becoming a reality.

Here's a simple analogy that illustrates what churches must do to incorporate more than 20–25 percent of their active membership into ministry. Every person reading this book has tried to lose weight or knows someone that has tried. An "expert" tells a person that to lose weight long term, he must exercise and cut down on the daily amount of calories consumed. Four months later, the expert sees the overweight person at the health club. The expert politely asks how the program has gone. The overweight person sarcastically responds, "Obviously it did not work; I am eight pounds heavier than when we talked four months ago." The expert inquires about the two main requirements to lose weight (exercise and lowering food consumption). The overweight person states that he has worked out four days a week and also lowered food consumption drastically.

A friend who is standing beside the overweight person laughs and says, "You could not lose weight just based on what we eat for lunch four or five days a week. Even if you fasted between meals, you would still be taking in more calories than required to lose weight."

A little further probing by the expert reveals that the overweight person was incorporating one lifestyle change (exercise) while not incorporating the other necessary change (food consumption). At the end of the conversation, the overweight person agrees that he **thought** he had changed his eating habits, but in reality he was still overeating. He agrees that proper diet, along with exercise, would have to be incorporated **simultaneously** and measured to achieve the desired weight loss results.

I, along with thousands of churches across America, **thought** that if we could create the proper tool to help believers **identify** how and where to do ministry, along with a process to get them to proper ministries, then the problem would be solved with regard to why "only 10 percent of American church members are involved in any kind of personal ministry" (Warren 1995, pp. 365–366).

I have been working in my own church for over 10 years in **connecting** members into ministry. I have traveled thousands of miles across America and overseas listening to thousands of ministers and churches struggle to change the paradigm of only a few members doing all the ministry. I have searched the Scriptures for insights, along with conferences, books and seemingly every available means to discover how to get more than 10–20 percent of members involved in ministry.

In 2004, I began to vaguely understand some of the problems churches were having with regard to member assimilation. Then in 2005, the lights went on and I had my aha moment in understanding the problem. I quickly went from glee, in clearly seeing the issues facing the church in this area, to panic, when it became clear from God what my next assignment was to be for the Church. My assignment would be to help churches **evaluate** how good they were at incorporating the six elements (discussed in this book) and develop **practical** resources to help them raise their level of effectiveness with regard to the six elements. I had to ask myself a difficult question, "Are You Committed to the difficult assignment?" This book, along with the resources that have and will be developed, are my response to the challenge that God has laid before me!

The six elements that must be incorporated **simultaneously** to increase ministry servants within our churches are a commitment to **connecting**, **identifying**, **equipping**, **empowering**, **encouraging** and **multiplying**. These six words will be thoroughly developed in the following pages. You must ask yourself, "Are You Committed?" to move beyond a philosophical agreement with these six elements to experientially incorporating them within your church and/or ministry. My desire is that you, like me, will answer with a resounding YES! I look forward to hearing from many of you regarding the powerful results of committing and **simultaneously** implementing these six elements to **connect** God's people in meaningful ministry.

Before You Begin: Take Note of Terminology

In the pages that follow, it will become obvious that the words below have incredible significance for this book. For this reason, all of these words are in bold throughout this book to bring attention to their importance in the concepts presented. The number in parentheses denotes the number of times the word is used within the book.

Connect (36)
Connecting (72)
Connected (14)
Connection (2)

Identify (53)
Identifying (44)
Identified (6)
Identification (5)
Identifies (5)

Equip (78)
Equipping (106)
Equipped (35)
Equipper (30)

Empower (38)
Empowered (24)
Empowering (61)
Empowerment (18)
Empowers (1)

Encourage (45)
Encouragement (79)

Encouraging (56)
Encouraged (21)
Encourages (23)
Encourager (2)

Multiply (17)
Multiplied (5)
Multiplying (38)
Multiplication (10)
Multiplies (1)

The phrase "God's People" in the title of the book will be used interchangeably with these other phrases throughout the book.

- church members
- believers
- volunteers
- Christians
- attendees
- regular attendees
- ministry servants
- ministry workers

In each case, the specific phrase used is the one I thought would be most appropriate for the context it is being used in. There could have been other phrases, such as "Christ follower," "disciple of Christ" or many others, that are used by various segments of Christendom. Words and phrases often carry different meanings, even when the same idea is being conveyed. As a result, sometimes readers can't fully grasp the idea or concept because of the language a specific word or phrase conveys to them personally. Therefore, I highly recommend that wherever one of the preceding words is used throughout this book, just substitute whatever phrase you would use in referring to that word.

Is the Church on Steroids?

W hat do many athletes and churches have in common? On the surface, maybe not much. However, I have concluded that both have followed a similar course for **short-term results** with little regard for **long-term consequences**. Both have replaced hard work with shortcuts to improve immediate performance.

Most reading this book are now saying, "Where are you coming from with this analogy?" Before clarifying the analogy, let me explain what is believed to have started in the 1950s with athletes. **Athletes in the 1950s began to be introduced to steroids and realized they could perform at higher levels by taking steroids.**

The first well-known athlete to go public regarding steroid use was feared defensive lineman Lyle Alzado, who played 15 years in the NFL with the Denver Broncos, Cleveland Browns and Oakland Raiders. For years, he denied using steroids. In July of 1991, he came clean in a story for *Sports Illustrated*. Seven years after playing his last football game, he died from brain lymphoma, a rare form of brain cancer. While there is no hard evidence that he developed brain cancer from taking steroids, Alzado was convinced steroids led to the brain cancer and his short life of 43 years.

The steroid scandal became well-known in 2005 with the investigation of major league baseball players. As of the writing of this book, most will conclude we still do not fully know the harmful ramifications steroids will have on those who have utilized them. Therefore, the consequences of what started in the 1950s may not be fully understood until 60–70 years later.

Now, back to the analogy between athletes and churches. In the late 1970s and early 1980s, churches began to take shortcuts to increase performance primarily in one area—worship attendance. If my theory is right—in that church leaders begin pumping steroids (figuratively speaking) into the church to increase attendance—we may not realize the consequences of an impotent Church until 60 or 70 years later, if we even acknowledge the consequences or the reasons for the consequences. What could make this even more difficult to recognize would be failing to understand the harmful impact of focusing on one mission objective of the Church, to the detriment of the other objectives. At least with steroids and athletes, today there is a consensus that they are harmful to one's body.

How many times is there a lack of agreement on what has caused negative consequences? For a prime example, look no further than our government and the perspective between Democrats and Republicans when it comes to the impact of President Roosevelt's and Lyndon Johnson's creating and handling of welfare. Most would agree that society is no further along today in eliminating the welfare system than it was before Johnson's measures in the 1960s. Many would even argue that we are worse off today than when the programs were put in place to eliminate welfare. However, there is debate after debate on who and what brought us to the place we are today and how to solve the problems of welfare. Sadly, the same arguments could be debated on who and why the Church in America is losing influence and impact on society today.

I believe passionately that focusing on one mission objective (worship) to the detriment of the others (discipleship, evangelism, fellowship and ministry) is causing the Church in North America to lose impact and therefore not be able to influence those without Christ that Jesus is the answer to challenges facing individuals and society. Keep in mind, I did not state a church or several churches are losing influence, but *the* Church. A gifted speaker with dynamic worship can fill a huge parking lot that flows into a big room (worship services), but I for one do not equate a church that reaches large numbers of people the same as the Church impacting and changing lives throughout North America. Filling a large room for worship services does not equate to long-term impact on future generations.

Before writing me off, consider the words of 2 Timothy 4:3 which state, "For the time will come when men will not put up with sound doctrine. Instead, to suit their own desires, they will gather around them a great number of teachers to say what their itching ears want to hear." Could that time be now? Could the focus on **moralistic** (do the right thing), **therapeutic** (feel good about yourself), **deism** (it's about me) that is taught in many church worship services today be the warning Paul is giving Timothy in 2 Timothy 4:3? Could it possibly be that many calling themselves Bible-believing evangelicals have succumbed to 2 Timothy 4:3 all in the name of being relevant? Does this type of worship lead to a weak, anemic Church?

Purpose and Mission of the Church

Let me move away from my steroids analogy and give what most would consider the fivefold purpose of the Church. I will refer to the fivefold mission of the church instead of purpose of the Church. "Purpose" is **why** we exist and "mission" is **how** we fulfill purpose. The purpose of the Church is to glorify God. How (mission) the Church glorifies God is through worship, evangelism, discipleship, fellowship and ministry (see Figure 1.1).

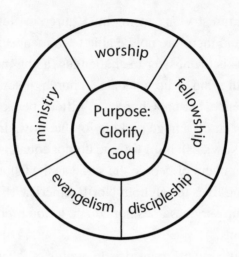

Figure 1.1

I would agree that if you are doing one (i.e., evangelism) it should equate to impacting the others (i.e., discipleship, ministry, fellowship and worship). All five (worship, evangelism, discipleship, fellowship and ministry) are important because the Bible teaches the importance of all five. If you are teaching someone how to do evangelism, it is impacting the others. However, if you isolated each one and had to put every activity of a church in one of the five mission objectives, I submit worship would be the one that over the past 20 years has received the majority of resources. Volumes could be written on why this has taken place. However, for this book, I am going to briefly delve into the conclusion that the worship mission objective receives the majority of time and resources.

How Do We Glorify God?

First, we have to define what it means to "glorify God," which is the purpose of the Church. W. E. Vine's *Expository Dictionary of Old and New Testament Words* (1996) describes "glorify" as "ascribing honor to Him" (God). There are countless ways to ascribe honor to God. If we simplify how we ascribe honor to God, it would be through our words, actions and attitudes in living as God would desire a Christian to live. The Bible tells us to "...follow the example of Christ" (1 Corinthians 11:1). So how did Christ live? He came to save sinners–1 Timothy 1:15 (evangelism), create fellowship among followers–Matthew 26:17–30 (fellowship), teach believers God's way to live–Luke 11:1 (discipleship), worship the Father–John 4:10 (worship) and serve others–Matthew 20:28 (ministry). Therefore, **how** (mission) we glorify God (**why** we are here–purpose) is through evangelism, fellowship, discipleship, worship and ministry. Acts 2:42–47 refers to all five mission objectives being fulfilled from the start of the church in Jerusalem.

Why Don't Churches Balance Mission Objectives?

It only takes a casual observance of churches to realize most overemphasize one or two of the mission objectives above the others. I did not state that they ignored the others, but that they overemphasized one or two to the minimal emphasis of the others. I am sure if you asked most of these churches if they overemphasized one or two mission objectives over others, many would not even be aware of this disparity. Others would claim, and even justify, and give instances where they were balanced.

Today, it is popular to brag about saying no to almost everything as it relates to ministry. Often these churches come across as arrogant as to why they "do" so little. Secondly, they are very convincing as to why they do so little. Thirdly, they are influencing countless churches across America to do so little, to the detriment of Christianity's influence.

Many senior pastors and church leaders only focus on the objective(s) that *they* are passionate about. They make the decisions on what others in the church should or should not be exposed to. They flaunt that if you do not like that particular direction, find another church. They downplay the other objectives and justify

> *In most churches, more time and energy has been placed by the senior pastor on the weekly worship experience, than on the four other mission objectives of the church combined!*

why they focus on the ones they choose. If this was brought up to them, the majority would deny, and even compellingly and convincingly defend, why they do what they do.

Several years ago, there was an article in the *Harvard Business Review* about a study done on CEO's of major corporations. The study concluded most of the CEO's had little self awareness. Just because someone can grow something (business or church) big, does not mean they have good awareness of measures that are or are not implemented that ultimately cause the business or church to be unhealthy in the long term.

In most churches, more time and energy has been placed by the senior pastor on the weekly worship experience, than on the four other mission objectives of the church *combined!*

Is North America Repeating History?

In gathering material for this book, I had a conversation with a church history professor from a leading seminary within the United States. I asked him to tell me some major features of Christianity in Europe in the 19th century. He gave many interesting insights—one being the beautiful church buildings that were filled many times over to hear preachers like Charles Spurgeon. I asked my professor friend if the following theory had any validity or was totally ludicrous and without merit. He thought there might be some merit to my theory.

My theory is that **part** of the fall of Christianity's influence in Europe can be attributed to focusing too much on one of the mission objectives (worship/preaching) to the detriment of the others.

There have been numerous books on the reasons Christianity has become so anemic in its impact on society in Europe. I do not disagree on what others have stated as to the reasons for the decline of Christianity's influence in Europe. However, I would like to add that focusing too much on just one aspect of the mission of the church (worship/preaching) is also contributing to its decline. I am afraid that with so much emphasis on "the big room" where worship takes place, that the Church in North America may be traveling down the road Europe has traveled, resulting in Christianity having little impact on society. One needs to look no further than church history to see what happens to Christianity's impact and influence when the ministry by the people is replaced by professionals and a "big show."

I know what the critics are saying about the way much of contemporary church is done today with regard to the ministry objective. But we **empower** our members in small groups to fulfill the ministry aspect of the church. The same critics would agree that leadership flows from the top. You can't—but for the sake of argument, suppose you could—measure through thoughts and actions the exact amount of time and energy a senior pastor devotes to planning and implementing ways for members to fulfill ministry to both fellow believers and non-believers. I am convinced the gauge would not register a substantial portion of their time and energy. However, if you put the gauge on the time spent on bringing people into "the big room" for worship, the gauge would register extremely high.

Back to the New Testament Church

The words "love" and "one" and "another" are referenced 17 times in the New Testament. The context for the use of these three words is in reference from one believer to another. This does not even include the countless passages like Acts 2:42–47 where the believers meet together *daily* to fellowship, give to those in need among each other and praise God. I sincerely believe that if a gauge could have been placed on the early church leaders, they would be far more balanced than the church leaders today in fulfilling the five mission objectives (worship, evangelism, fellowship, discipleship and ministry). Leaders in the early church did not spend so much time creating irresistible environments for the unchurched to hear the gospel. They did not spend so much time and energy convincing fellow believers why it was necessary to create these irresistible environments to cater to the unchurched. Notice I did not state they were unconcerned about non-Christians. The leaders of the early church created irresistible environments where love was so evident among believers that unbelievers could not resist what the early church offered to those within the fellowship. This irresistible love was developed through ministering one to another through TIME together.

This book is not focusing on worship, but rather on briefly highlighting the ramifications of expending too much focus, resources and energy on worship to the detriment of the other four mission objectives of the Church—fellowship, evangelism, discipleship and ministry. If you are interested in understanding the current state of worship, Marva J. Dawn has written an excellent book: *Reaching Out Without Dumbing Down – A Theology of Worship for This Urgent Time* (1995). Furthermore, the focus of my writing this book is not primarily about the mission objectives of worship, discipleship, fellowship and evangelism, but about why the *ministry* mission objective needs to be formulated for churches. Also, it is about how to formulate ministry principles and practical initiatives around ministry within the church. Again, doing one objective should impact the others, but we are isolating the ministry objective in this book. Before laying the groundwork for incorporating new practices within churches as it relates to ministry, we needed to understand the current place the ministry objective has within the Church.

Pertinent Questions Regarding Emphasis on Worship

- Do you agree that more emphasis is placed on the weekly worship experience compared to the other four objectives (discipleship, evangelism, fellowship and ministry)?

- Do you agree that placing more emphasis on the worship experience is the most effective way to reach non-Christians?

- Do you agree that placing more emphasis on the worship experience is the most effective way to keep believers involved in church?

- Why might churches place a greater emphasis on the weekly worship experience?

- What might be some unhealthy consequences of placing too much emphasis on the worship experience—to the detriment of the other four mission objectives?

- Should one mission objective have a greater emphasis than the others? Why or why not?

- Will emphasizing the worship experience create a healthy future for the ongoing impact of Christianity? Why or why not?

Where Do We Begin?

Dr. Henry Blackaby has impacted millions of believers worldwide with his workbook *Experiencing God* and the resources that have been developed around this workbook. Years before working through the workbook, I knew one phrase about *Experiencing God*: "find out where God is working and join Him." The premise behind *Experiencing God* is for God's people to look out over the world and join God in what He is doing to reach the world with the message of Christ's redeeming love.

While I do not want to criticize this approach, I would like to add a step before looking outward. To **connect** God's people to meaningful ministry, the beginning point should be looking inward at who he/she is to **identify** where to serve as the feet and hands of God's redemptive love.

I am not an expert theologian, but I have learned a few theological truths. One is: there will always be more needs than there are people to meet those needs. We live in a fallen world. Christ did not meet every emotional, spiritual and physical need during His earthly ministry. Why do God's people sometimes think we can meet every need we encounter? The place for God's people to begin in ministry is knowing and understanding themselves both corporately and individually.

Why on Earth Am I Here?

Rick Warren was already well-known before writing *The Purpose Driven Life* (2002) with the tag line "Why on earth am I here?" He has become almost a household name in many circles since the publication of his bestselling book. I am amused how many church leaders agree with Warren's premise that God has a unique purpose for each believer **until** they need to fill slots within the organization of their churches. Then, it becomes serve wherever you are needed for the good of the Kingdom. These leaders feel if greeters are needed, then greet. If nursery workers are needed, then serve in the nursery with a glad heart. These same leaders will turn around and profess how they serve according to their *strengths*. However, without directly stating it, they believe members should serve only where there are *needs*.

I recently read a book by a well-known pastor who wrote about leadership and how he allocates his time around leading the church through his strengths. The same pastor does a message each year that convinces the members to serve wherever they are needed. I submit that if a volunteer has a limited amount of time to give directly to eternal causes, it would be even more important to serve according to his/her strengths and not just where they are needed.

80/20 Rule

The 80/20 Rule states: 20 percent of the people do 80 percent of the ministry. Churches need to introduce the 80/20 Rule for individual believers to incorporate into their decisions on *where* to serve within the local church and outside the walls of the church. The 80/20 Rule proposes that churches should first help God's people **identify** where they are competent and passionate in ministry. Then, churches should help them determine their available time for ministry. The Rule helps God's people spend 80 percent of their available ministry time serving within their strengths, competence and passion and 20 percent where there are needs within the church.

Andy Stanley says in *The Next Generation Leader* (2003, p. 45), "Recognize that you have limited strengths. Do whatever it takes to discover what they are. Once you know, find a work environment that allows you to focus your energies on the few things you were created to do well." Stanley's statement is equally true for God's people—whether they are the senior pastor, custodian in a high school, public school teacher, lawyer or whatever—when it comes to seeking their place to serve within the local church or outside the local church, wherever God has them serving.

An example would be a person who determines they have five hours per week to volunteer at their local church. Four hours should be served in their competence and passion areas and the other hour wherever the church has a need. The hours may or may not be distributed equally in a given year. In this example, a volunteer who gave five hours each week could volunteer approximately 260 hours per year, 52 of which would be given to wherever the church had a need (i.e., nursery), regardless of competence or passion.

What Goes Around Comes Around

The 1950s ushered in a new movement within churches in America. Church programming, with volunteers to lead the programming, was birthed. Prior to the '50s, churches may have offered Sunday School to the children, but not much in the way of programs for adults. As the programming grew, churches had to find more and more volunteers to fill slots. Basically, churches created the programs and then found people to fill the slots, regardless of competence or passion. We know what happened with this type of programming. Church members burned out in churches all over America. Bill Hybels captured this burnout in his book *The Volunteer Revolution*. He states,

"But after five years of serving with abandon, great people started flaming out. Men and women with pure hearts and deep devotion said, 'I can't do this anymore. I'm exhausted.' Others said, 'I'm angry. What you're asking isn't reasonable.' Some left the church so wounded that they had to get away to recover.

"But as the decade of the '70s turned to the '80s, we realized there was more to faithful servanthood than just working harder. We had to move back toward the concept of spiritual gifts we had learned in the youth ministry.

"We started teaching the concept of giftedness every way we could. We developed an in-depth spiritual gift assessment course called *Network*, which we taught throughout the year on Saturdays. We taught a nine-week series on spiritual gifts at our midweek services. We even came up with an abbreviated spiritual gift assessment that I used at our weekend services.

"During the '80s, many people in our congregation discovered the exhilaration of serving in an area of perfect fit, where their personality, passions, and spiritual gifts all matched their volunteer role. But we ran into two problems . . . People knew their identity as servants and wanted to serve, but knowing how and where to serve had become a very complicated process." (2004, pp. 69–70)

Obviously, Hybels has a better perspective to claim that the process referred to above encountered problems at Willow Creek where he serves as senior pastor. I would disagree with him that the solution was to throw away the intentional **identification** process (*Network*) in helping members discover their optimal place of service. I can't claim to know all the dynamics that caused the process to return inadequate results for his church, but I can affirm that I have seen hundreds of churches encounter the same problems Hybels found at Willow Creek with an **identification** process. The answer is not to throw the baby (intentional processes like *Network*) out with the bath water (how members get **connected** in ministry). The answer is in recognizing that helping members **identify** their uniqueness in Christ through evaluations like personality, spiritual gifts and abilities assessments is only the beginning of a "very complicated process," as he calls it. When we stop short of incorporating the other elements of the process that this book proposes—**equipping, empowering, encouraging** and **multiplying**—then we don't end up with a "complicated process," but an *incomplete* process that leads to failure.

> *Attending worship services and being involved in a small group are essential to the health of a church and its members. However, focusing on only two aspects of what the body of believers are supposed to be will lead to the demise of the power of the Church to impact society.*

The program-based movement gained speed through the '80s and into the '90s with society's emphasis on choices. Look no further than church consultant Lyle Schaller's book, *The-Seven-Day-A-Week Church* (1992). To have a seven-day-a-week church requires lots and lots of volunteers with lots and lots of organization and coordination. The program-based movement seems to have peaked as of the writing of this book. Could it possibly be that church leaders who have abandoned important ministries were swept up with the trend and did not really believe that those serving were possibly being the hands and feet of Jesus to a world that desperately needs His touch? The trend has been replaced by what I call " The One-Hour-A-Week Church." Maybe a well-known church leader will one day write a book called *The One-Hour-A-Week Church* that presents a compelling case for why God's people should only focus on attending church for one hour. Better yet, maybe one entitled *The Two-Hour-A-Week Church* so we can make room for small groups that have become so popular.

Attending worship services and being involved in a small group are essential to the health of a church and its members. However, focusing on only two aspects of what the body of believers are supposed to be will lead to the demise of the power of the Church to impact society.

Somewhere between the program-based model that attempts to be everything to everyone and the contemporary model that offers little except to bring people together in a big room (worship), there is the balance. Church history, along with history in general, is full of people who have reacted to a pendulum swing in one direction, only to swing the pendulum in an entirely different direction. A commitment to balance must first start with God's people individually. However, individuality is never the goal, but the launching point, to help God's people live in community and reach those without Christ. The following six chapters will provide a balance when it comes to focusing on the individual, and then moving the individual to focus on others.

Questions for Further Thought

- Does your church keep accurate records of the percent of members involved in ministry?

- Does your church provide too many programs or too few programs for members and non-members to engage in? What are some reasons for your answer?

- Does your church seek to provide balance regarding members serving according to their competency and passion versus where the church has needs? Give examples or lack of examples for your answer.

- Do most members within your church serve according to their competency or passion, or wherever there is a need, regardless of their competency or passion? Explain your answer.

- Does your church intentionally recruit people who are best suited for programs before starting the programs, or does it start the programs and then find the workers? Give examples if you can for your answer.

Committed to Connecting God's People to Meaningful Ministry

Interviewer: Are you committed to **connecting** God's people into ministry at your church?

Pastor: That is a silly question. Of course I am. Why, without members doing ministry, there would be very little ministry.

Interviewer: Pastor, do you believe every member/believer is a minister?

Pastor: Yes. The priesthood of the believer teaches that every believer is a minister?

Interviewer: Who are the volunteers within your church?

Pastor: Those who are leaders.

Interviewer: Do 100% of your members serve in some capacity within your church?

Pastor: No.

Interviewer: What percentage of your members serve in some capacity within your church?

Pastor: Maybe 25%.

Interviewer: Why do you believe 75% of your members do not serve?

Pastor:	Many have a lack of commitment, others are lazy, while others are too busy and some do not realize the need.
Interviewer:	Could part of the problem be attributed to the church staff/ministry leadership?
Pastor:	I am not sure I understand what you are asking.
Interviewer:	Let me ask the question in another way. Would it be fair to assume almost all of your church staff/ministry leaders' time is invested in **recruiting** five-talent individuals (as Matthew 25:15 teaches)?
Pastor:	That would be a fair assumption.
Interviewer:	Could it possibly be that you and your staff/ministry leaders do not take the responsibility that you are part of the reason the majority of your members do not serve in ministry?
Pastor:	This interview is over.

Problem

For the sake of this hypothetical interview, the pastor abruptly ending the interview was an easy way to end it. Another direction the interview could have taken would be an argument as to why the church was **connecting** such a small percentage of its members to ministry. The hypothetical interview is not meant to create an argument, but to point out a glaring weakness and challenge the church is facing today with how it does church. This weakness and challenge is not new, but has been around for longer than anyone who is reading this book. However, the future of the church's relevancy may depend on correcting the weakness and overcoming the challenge—not to mention the biblical mandate to do church differently than we currently do it. The Church in North America may drift into irrelevancy if it does not learn how to incorporate God's people into meaningful ministry.

Wrestling with an Intentional Strategy

What keeps you up at night? If you asked a thousand senior pastors what they worry about (I know worry is not allowed to be part of a Christian's vocabulary) with regard to their churches, what would be their top responses? I suspect some answers would be the following:

- individuals without Christ
- finances of the church
- conflict within the church
- marriages that are struggling
- Sunday morning messages
- ability to cast vision
- hiring the right staff
- attendance
- social issues in society
- desire to be biblically sound while culturally relevant

I doubt many pastors would say, "To help every member of my church to be involved in ministry." Many churches claim on their church bulletin "every member a minister," but we all know that what we say does not always match what we do.

My spiritual father taught me a saying early on in my Christian life. He said,

> *"Your walk talks and your talk talks, but your walk talks louder than your talk talks ."*

"Your walk talks and your talk talks, but your walk talks louder than your talk talks."

If you think the statement is hard to read, try saying it—what a tongue twister! Even better, ponder the situation as it relates to "every member a minister" and how it relates to your church's intentional strategy for **connecting** every member in ministry that attends your church. A simple way to phrase the statement is in a question: Do you have an intentional strategy for **connecting** every member or regular attendee at your church into ministry? Notice the question does not state **connecting** every member or regular attendee into ministry *within the walls* of your church. More will be developed later regarding where your church helps members and regular attendees get **connected** into ministry.

Actions Reveal Beliefs

A staff member recently told me about a conversation with his senior pastor. The staff member was trying to get his senior pastor to implement a process I have developed called *Finding Your PLACE in Ministry.* The pastor responded to the staff member, "I don't want us to have to be committed to finding a place for every member to serve who goes through the process."

I was taken aback when I heard the statement. I know many pastors' actions reflect the statement, but I had not heard one actually state it that bluntly. I suspect if that senior pastor were asked if he believed in the priesthood of the believer, he would emphatically say yes. I also suspect if you asked him what are the responsibilities of him and his staff, he would say, "Among other responsibilities, to **equip** the saints (members) for the work of ministry." If you posed the question, "Do you believe 20–30 percent of your members should be participants in ministry while the other 70–80 percent should be spectators?" what do you think his answer would be? My guess is he would say no. Yet in his case, his actions and even his words, reveal his true beliefs.

I know many of my readers and some who wax elegant on stools as communicators leading church conferences could rip apart the previous example as to why only 20–30 percent serve within a church. They could present a compelling case as to why the participation is and should be 20–30 percent. This book is not meant to debate these well-meaning individuals, but to offer a different perspective than the one they communicate, often by default. The perspective they communicate as it relates to **connecting** God's people to ministry may not be directly taught, but it is indirectly caught!

The Future of the North American Church

I propose the future of the Church in North America hinges partly on how serious its leaders believe and act upon the command to "**equip** the saints for the work of the ministry" (Ephesians 4:12). If church leaders do not change their primary focus from incorporating strategies to fill up "the big room" (worship services), then the future for my two small children and all children, as it relates to the church and its influence in society, will be vastly diminished. If church leaders continue to be swayed by compelling communicators set on allocating most resources to fill up the big room—to the exclusion of "doing ministry"—then the Church is headed to irrelevancy. An unchanged future for those who will never enter into a relationship with God will become a greater probability.

The purpose of this book is not to have church leaders abandon what they are doing, but to incorporate more balanced strategies in the allocation of time and resources in its mission of bringing Jesus to the world. If you personally do not impact the decisions of your church directly, you can incorporate the most powerful resource you have for change—prayer. Start praying for those within your church who are the decision-makers. Think about this famous quote by Edward Everett Hale:

I am only one, but I am one.
I cannot do everything, but I can do something.
And what I can do I will do.
And what I will do by the grace of God I shall do.

Remember, God has not called you to do everything, but He has called you to do something.

Where Did the Church Go Wrong?

Even a casual reading of the New Testament reveals some simple truths regarding ministry involvement by God's people. God created **every** believer for a purpose (Ephesians 2:10). He has **equipped every** believer with a spiritual gift(s) to fulfill His purpose (1 Corinthians 12:7 and Ephesians 4:7). God expects every believer to "use whatever gift he has received to serve others" (1 Peter 4:10). Why would almost every church leader agree with these statements intellectually, but do so little intentionally to allow every believer to experientially practice these truths?

Where did intellectual assent depart from experiential reality? In AD 313, the Church made a radical departure from its early beginnings. Emperor Constantine I issued the Edict of Milan declaring the Church no longer persecuted, but officially accepted. Up until this point, there was no distinction between clergy and laity. Churches were in homes, not the beautiful edifices that began to be built once Christianity became credible. Christians were all considered equal when it came to participating in worship, reaching those with Christ, edifying and building one another up and serving each other. It all changed with buildings. After the "first flurry of church buildings in 323-327, we ceased being an interactive family and turned into an audience. Spectators." (Rutz 1992, p. 9)

The Church went downhill after the Edict of Milan. Corruption, loss of biblical integrity and worldly power came to describe the Church. Yes, Martin Luther and those of the Reformation restored the Word of God to the people of God, but not the work of God. The priesthood of the believer was restored in doctrine, but not in practice.

Solution

The seeds of what men like Martin Luther and John Calvin started were watered little by little through the next four centuries. During the sixteenth and seventeenth centuries, the Puritans cultivated the teachings of the Bible regarding ministry by the laity for the people. The eighteenth century saw men like John and Charles Wesley scatter seed to help the people recapture the teachings of the Bible, while the nineteenth century saw the revival preachers and missionaries begin to help believers understand the importance of a personal relationship with God. The twentieth century saw the birth of the Pentecostal movement, where many of its leaders did not have formal training, but were used by God in powerful ways.

In the mid-twentieth century, seminary professors began to write each other about spiritual gifts and their relevancy for every believer. Naturally, most common people could not understand what they were writing. Case in point—Dr. Dewey Todd, a friend of mine, while working on his doctorate was actually told by his dissertation committee that his paper was too simple and could be understood by common people.

In my research, Peter Wagner and Larry Gilbert have been two of the most instrumental people in the last 40 years in helping the Church understand that every believer is gifted and expected to use their gift(s). For many years, Wagner taught at Fuller Theological Seminary where he developed a following among both charismatic and non-charismatic circles relating to the use of spiritual gifts among all believers. Gilbert was from the east coast and had a great deal of influence among more conservative-fundamentalist church leaders. There was a song that came out several years ago entitled, "I Was Country When Country Wasn't Cool." Peter Wagner and Larry Gilbert were proponents of "every member a minister" before it became popular and "cool" to teach about spiritual gifts in the middle to late 1980s.

The 1980s saw a business model that has been termed "**empowerment**" catch on in the church world in the late '80s to early '90s. Two well-known pastors, Bill Hybels and Rick Warren became proponents of this **empowerment** model by developing an intentional strategy for **connecting** believers to ministry. They incorporated not only spiritual gifts, but personality, passion, abilities and life experiences, to help their members find meaningful service within their churches. Other churches and ministries, like the one I am a part of, came along in the '90s and into the twenty-first century to champion and resource churches into helping members **identify** places to serve within the church. Little by little, the Church has been moving toward God's original plan that every believer is a minister.

Putting the Cart before the Horse

The late '90s ushered in my involvement in the movement to restore the priesthood of the believer from intellectual assent to practical reality. My official engagement into **connecting** God's people into ministry started in 1998. I learned a great deal from 1998 to 2004. In my initial study, I learned what went wrong, starting with Constantine up to the current situation. I began addressing the glaring problem of believers **identifying** their uniqueness for ministry. I developed a process called PLACE to help God's people **identify** how God has uniquely **equipped** them for ministry. In 2004, I realized four other truths not being sufficiently addressed by churches in **connecting** God's people into meaningful ministry. The truths revolved around learning not only how to **identify** believers for ministry, but also the need to **equip** ministry leaders and for ministry leaders to **empower** believers for ministry. Also, once members are **equipped**, most do not receive intentional **encouraging** within their ministry. Finally, I learned there is a glaring lack of attention given to **multiplying** believers for ministry.

We had become so focused on helping the individual church member **identify** their God-given design, competency and passion for ministry that we failed to address the other aspects of members **connecting** in ministry. We did not realize the role staff and ministry leaders played in turning members into ministers. While we may all agree that our efforts to turn members into ministers have not produced the results we desired, we may disagree on why the results have been inadequate. Most church leaders have pointed to *complicated* processes or claimed the resources utilized were the wrong resources. Rarely will you find church leaders who point to incompetence on behalf of staff or ministry leaders to **equip**, **empower**, **encourage** and **multiply** God's people for ministry.

I was driving to the airport with a denominational leader who works in human resources for an agency with several hundred employees. I asked him what a typical day was like for him. He pointed to conflict resolution between supervisors and their staff. He told me that often supervisors want to fire a staff member under them for lack of performance—so they claim. What this human resource manager has discovered is lack of performance has often been caused by lack of supervision and training. He noted, "I have learned this is the way many of them behaved when working on a church staff. These former church staff members never learned how to train those they supervised."

Instead of blaming the inadequate results on a *complicated process,* maybe we should blame it on being *half-hearted* in committing to **connect** believers or on an *incomplete process* with *inadequate training* for **identifying**, **equipping**, **empowering**, **encouraging** and **multiplying**.

Why don't staff/ministry leaders **identify**, **equip**, **empower**, **encourage** and **multiply**?

• They have never been trained how to **identify**, **equip**, **empower**, **encourage** and **multiply** members for ministry.

• They are unaware they are not incorporating these elements adequately.
• They incorrectly believe they are adequately **identifying, equipping, empowering, encouraging** and **multiplying** members for ministry.
• They have consciously or unconsciously assessed that they do not have adequate time to do their current responsibilities, ensure that every member find his/her place in ministry and also provide training for that ministry.
• Their self-worth is contingent on doing ministry and not giving ministry to others.

The solution to this problem is found in Rick Warren's teachings. Warren believes the staff of a church (and may I add the ministry leaders) are to be the *administrators* while the members are to be the *ministers* (1995).

I agree there is much talk and many books written regarding these five words (**identifying, equipping, empowering, encouraging** and **multiplying**), but little doing in living out these five words simultaneously and holistically in churches. Will you ask yourself, "Are you a doer of the Word or merely a hearer who deceives even yourself?" (James 1:22) If you are a ministry leader, are you an **equipper**? Are you one who **identifies, empowers, encourages** and **multiplies** God's people for meaningful ministry?"

The Evolution of the Ideal Intentional Process

I coined my learning of the principles in this book as "Putting the Cart before the Horse." This is my story of learning this saying the hard way as it relates to **equipping** ministry leaders to **empower** believers for ministry. I hope in reading this book you will not make the same mistakes I did in my early days by only **identifying** members for ministry. If you are like me and have made these mistakes, I hope this book will **encourage** and challenge you to commit to a holistic approach to **connecting** God's people to ministry.

In 1998, I was asked to join the staff of Council Road Baptist Church in Bethany, Oklahoma. My title was Associate Pastor of Ministry Development. In a nutshell, my job was to **connect** members into ministry at Council Road, thereby helping close the back door. Mark Hartman, the senior pastor, gave me total freedom to fulfill this task in any fashion I could while getting the job done. I spent over a year traveling to other churches, attending conferences, reading and talking with church leaders and members about assimilating members into ministry. After all the research, I decided to create our own resources to help our members **identify** their unique design and a process to **connect** them to ministries. These resources were not only used at Council Road, but have now been utilized by over 4,000 churches, mainly in the United States. They have been used to a small degree in other countries as well.

The first workshop at Council Road was completed in March of 1999. We had about 35 individuals complete the workshop. Most were members, and a few had not yet joined the church. We trained six members to sit down one-on-one with those who completed all five sessions. In a one-on-one consultation, we determined the ministry areas for these individuals to pursue within our church. My office referred these individuals to the ministerial staff to follow up and hopefully incorporate into their ministries. The process up to this point was working beautifully. The individuals who attended the workshop and had their one-on-one consultations were motivated and energized to pursue opportunities within our church.

After the consultations, the motivation quickly dissipated for many of those who attended the workshop. Some were not followed up on by the staff member they were referred to. Others were thrown into a ministry area without understanding the commitment. Still others were inadequately trained or not trained at all within their ministry roles we **connected** them to. However, there were a few who were adequately trained for their new ministry responsibilities within the church. These individuals came away with a positive experience from the process. One new church member summed it up when a consultant suggested she serve in a certain ministry and she responded with, "I don't think I want to be referred to _____ (staff member's name blank to protect the guilty). I hear he never follows up with those referred to him."

Before you think too lowly of the staff I was serving on, let me share my own shortcomings in this process. I did not take the staff through the workbook "Finding Your PLACE in Ministry" until February of 2000, a year after taking over 200 members through the process. In other words, the staff members were getting assessment profiles of individuals while they did not even understand the language used within the profiles. For example, the "A" in PLACE stands for "Abilities Awareness." PLACE uses abilities, not as a person's skill or talents, but the ENVIRONMENT in which a person will be fulfilled and competent in serving within the church.

Our staff had no idea what the terms "realistic" or "conventional" abilities meant on the profile. While our staff fully supported my position to help members assimilate into ministry, they had no real clue what my position involved and what our tool—PLACE—or process was to accomplish this. The PLACE process and tool was to **identify** potential workers. The staff and ministry leaders were to determine if the individuals being referred met the requirements and wanted to fulfill the responsibilities of a ministry position. Also, it was up to the ministry leaders to **equip** those being referred to ministry positions. This was never communicated in written or verbal form. In February of 2000, we finally took our staff through the PLACE workshop and consultation training. Our challenges did not end there, but we were greatly improved.

To be honest, I did not realize the problem our process had created within the church until almost two years after leaving that staff position and moving back to Atlanta, Georgia. I knew we had struggles with the process, but I was also seeing some great successes with both individuals and ministries within our church.

However, thanks to Pastor Hartman's experiences, I became fully enlightened, not only to the depth of the problems with the process, but also to the solutions to the problems!

In November of 2002, Pastor Hartman moved from Council Road in Oklahoma to be the senior pastor of Sugar Creek Baptist Church in Sugarland, Texas. He served in 2003 as a member of my advisory board for PLACE Ministries. On December 2, 2003, I picked him up for our board meeting. He had been at Sugar Creek for one year, yet had not introduced PLACE at his church. (I know you're thinking, "And he is one of your board members!")

> *In looking back, I just assumed that staff and ministry leaders would know what to do with new workers. It was a wrong assumption.*

We briefly discussed our shortcomings about PLACE at Council Road and his desire to not replicate its shortcomings at Sugar Creek. As he stated to me, "At Council Road, we put the cart before the horse in our assimilation strategy." He said he needed to get the structure in place (no pun intended) before he introduced PLACE to the staff and then the members. He asked me if I had any books on building ministry teams, so we reviewed them in my home library that night. One book particularly piqued our interest. While on staff at Council Road, I was interviewed by George Barna for a book he was writing on building ministry teams. Pastor Hartman chose this book and took it with him.

Through experience, Pastor Hartman and I had discovered that taking members through the process before our staff experienced the process was indeed putting the cart before the horse. We recognized the weaknesses of not working first with our staff and ministry leaders so they would know how to incorporate (**equip**, **empower**, **encourage** and **multiply**) new workers into ministry teams. Not only did the Council Road staff not understand the language within the PLACE tool, but many did not know how to incorporate new individuals within their ministries. In looking back, I just assumed that staff and ministry leaders would know what to do with new workers. It was a wrong assumption.

I am excited to report how Pastor Hartman was able to successfully put the horse before the cart at Sugar Creek! So much was learned in this process from the results that took place the first year at Sugar Creek when the PLACE process was implemented correctly—with the horse before the cart.

The Process Improves…with Documented Success!

On Mark's flight back from the board meeting, he read the entire George Barna book, *The Power of Team Leadership* (2001), which addresses building ministry teams. He then ordered 60 copies of the book for his entire staff (including the custodial staff) to read during the first seven weeks of 2004. All 60 staff members met once a week for seven weeks to discuss two chapters at a time and how those concepts impacted them with regard to their jobs at Sugar Creek.

Following the seven weeks, the ministerial staff went away for a four-day retreat to discuss how they would intentionally incorporate new individuals into existing ministry teams they led within the church. Also, they established the goal that each ministerial staff member was to develop two new ministry areas within their respective ministry over the next year. Lastly, each staff member was given the responsibility of writing down every task they did to accomplish their ministry responsibilities. This detailed list would enable them to **identify** tasks they could delegate when **empowering** their members with ministry.

At the end of April in 2004, I spent two days with the Sugar Creek staff—all 60 of them, from the senior pastor to the custodial staff. During this time, I led them through the PLACE tool and taught them what comes after the self-discovery aspect. They were taught how to sit down with members one-on-one and help members process what they learned through the PLACE tool. Also, they learned how to assist members in determining possible ministry opportunities within the church.

In June of 2004, Pastor Hartman preached a series of messages that corresponded to member involvement in ministries. John Rushing, the minister of adult education, led their entire adult Bible study departments through the PLACE workbook during the Bible study hour at Sugar Creek. Since the initial introduction of PLACE to the entire church, John Rushing has led numerous other groups of smaller size through the PLACE process. I returned to Sugar Creek in August to train about 20 lay members how to conduct the one-on-one consultations.

The events above are really only the highlights of how Sugar Creek Baptist Church introduced an intentional strategy that used PLACE as a way to help members **identify** ministry opportunities. At the same time, they were preparing to introduce PLACE, staff members were writing descriptions of ministry opportunities to **empower** members for ministry. Also, they created a database in order to track members' involvement from the PLACE workshop to any ministries where they served.

Bottom line: What were the results of this intentional strategy for **connecting** members into meaningful ministry at Sugar Creek in 2004? They are numerous, but I will mention only two. First, when pastor Hartman became the senior pastor in 2002, the church was averaging about 1500 individuals attending Sunday services. By June of 2004, the church was averaging about 2500 individuals attending Sunday services. From June until December, over 450 new individuals were introduced to ministry opportunities for the first time at Sugar Creek. This is astounding even for a church the size of Sugar Creek. As of the writing of this book, Sugar Creek is averaging between 3500-4000 individuals attending Sunday services. **Connecting** God's people into meaningful ministry does grow churches!

Secondly, Sugar Creek exceeded its annual budget by over 15 percent. This was also astounding considering the budget was a multi-million dollar budget. People continually relay to me that they are not sure their church can expend the financial and personnel resources needed to intentionally implement a process to **connect** God's people to ministry. My reply to them is, "People give financially where they have their time and energy invested."

Are You Committed?

The remainder of the book will present a case for the need to commit to **connecting**, **identifying**, **equipping**, **empowering**, **encouraging** and **multiplying** believers for ministry. Will you commit to evaluating where you and your church are in incorporating these six principles? Will you consider committing to incorporating these six concepts into the DNA of your church or organization? Even if you are not a decision-maker within your church, will you commit to pray?

This book will present a compelling case for you to say yes to these commitments. Along the way, practical tools will be referenced to help you in implementing them. The first of these tools are two evaluations provided for assessing the effectiveness of either a church or an individual ministry in **connecting** God's people to meaningful ministry.

CONNECTING Evaluation Survey:
For A CHURCH

O O O

To take the evaluations and score yourself, look on the reverse side of the back jacket of this book. You will find a user ID and password. Go to this website: *http://www.mobilyzr.com/evaluations* and insert your user ID and password. Additional instructions are on the website. Once you are taking the evaluations on the website, the results will be graphed. In this book, you can review the evaluations, but not score yourself or those who take them as a group. Also, there is the opportunity to purchase evaluations and divide them into groups to also assess the effectiveness of various groups within your church or ministry regarding **connecting** God's people to meaningful ministry.

The evaluations are brief and simple, yet the results can be life-changing for you and your church. Invest just a few minutes of time so you can **identify** where you are and what your next steps need to be in **connecting**, **identifying**, **equipping**, **empowering**, **encouraging** and **multiplying** believers for ministry in YOUR church!

O O O

1. My church has a central list of every ministry worker within my church.

Yes ❑   No ❑   Not Sure ❑

2. My church provides an intentional process to help potential volunteers discover their competency and passion for ministry before **connecting** them to a ministry position.

Yes ❑   Some Ministries ❑   No ❑   Not Sure ❑

3. At least once per year, through preaching, my senior pastor emphasizes how and why a member should **connect** through serving within a ministry.

Yes ❑   No ❑   Not Sure ❑

4. My church provides specific training for anyone entering a ministry position.

Yes ❑   Some Ministries ❑   No ❑   Not Sure ❑

5. My church believes and practices "people first—programs second".

Strongly Agree ❑   Agree ❑   Somewhat Agree/Disagree ❑
Disagree ❑   Strongly Disagree ❑   Not Sure ❑

6. My church informs new members up front what is expected with regard to serving within the church.

Strongly Agree ❑   Agree ❑   Somewhat Agree/Disagree ❑
Disagree ❑   Strongly Disagree ❑   Not Sure ❑

7. My church has job descriptions for ministry opportunities within my church.

Every Ministry ❑   Most Ministries ❑   Some Ministries ❑
No Ministries ❑   Not Sure ❑

8. My church has the following percentage of its active adult members involved in ministry.

Over 50% ❑   35–49% ❑   20–34% ❑   10–19% ❑
Under 10% ❑

9. My church promotes "every member a minister."

Strongly Agree ❑   Agree ❑   Somewhat Agree/Disagree ❑
Disagree ❑   Strongly Disagree ❑   Not Sure ❑

10. My church has entry points for believers at various spiritual maturity levels to engage in ministry.

Strongly Agree ❑   Agree ❑   Somewhat Agree/Disagree ❑
Disagree ❑   Strongly Disagree ❑   Not Sure ❑

11. My church has a record of how many new ministry workers are added from year to year.

Yes ❑   No ❑   Not Sure ❑

12. My church values ministry involvement on the same level as worship, evangelism, discipleship or fellowship.

Strongly Agree ❑   Agree ❑   Somewhat Agree/Disagree ❑
Disagree ❑   Strongly Disagree ❑   Not Sure ❑

CONNECTING Evaluation Survey:
For A MINISTRY

O O O

1. My ministry has a central list of every ministry worker within my ministry.

   Yes ❑   No ❑   Not Sure ❑

2. My church provides an intentional process to help potential volunteers discover their competency and passion for ministry before **connecting** them to a ministry position.

   Yes ❑   Some Ministries ❑   No ❑   Not Sure ❑

3. At least once per year, through preaching, my senior pastor emphasizes how and why a member should **connect** through serving within a ministry.

   Yes ❑   No ❑   Not Sure ❑

4. My ministry leader provides specific training for anyone entering a ministry position.

   Yes ❑   Some Ministries ❑   No ❑   Not Sure ❑

5. My ministry leader believes and practices "people first— programs second".

   Strongly Agree ❑   Agree ❑   Somewhat Agree/Disagree ❑
   Disagree ❑   Strongly Disagree ❑   Not Sure ❑

6. My ministry leader informs new members up front what is expected with regard to serving within my ministry.

Strongly Agree ❑   Agree ❑   Somewhat Agree/Disagree ❑
Disagree ❑   Strongly Disagree ❑   Not Sure ❑

7. My ministry has written job descriptions for ministry opportunities within the ministry.

Every Ministry ❑   Most Ministries ❑   Some Ministries ❑
No Ministries ❑   Not Sure ❑

8. My ministry has a healthy balance of workers doing ministry versus those receiving ministry.

Strongly Agree ❑   Agree ❑   Somewhat Agree/Disagree ❑
Disagree ❑   Strongly Disagree ❑   Not Sure ❑

9. My ministry leader promotes "every member a minister."

Strongly Agree ❑   Agree ❑   Somewhat Agree/Disagree ❑
Disagree ❑   Strongly Disagree ❑   Not Sure ❑

10. My ministry has entry points for believers at various spiritual maturity levels to engage in ministry.

Strongly Agree ❑   Agree ❑   Somewhat Agree/Disagree ❑
Disagree ❑   Strongly Disagree ❑   Not Sure ❑

11. My ministry has a record of how many new ministry workers are added from year to year.

Yes ❑   No ❑   Not Sure ❑

12. My ministry values ministry involvement on the same level as worship, evangelism, discipleship or fellowship.

Strongly Agree ❏   Agree ❏   Somewhat Agree/Disagree ❏
Disagree ❏   Strongly Disagree ❏   Not Sure ❏

Committed to Identifying God's People for Meaningful Ministry

Process Not Product

Too often, we emphasize the product, downplay the process, and then wonder why we are not getting the results we intended with the product. The process is more important than the product or tool. The product is to enhance the process.

An example that is played out over and over again in churches is when they purchase spiritual gifts inventories and give them to the entire congregation, along with a sermon series at the same time by the senior pastor on spiritual gifts. Churches believe the product (spiritual gifts inventories), along with the event of a message or two, will create more workers for the church. If they stop to evaluate (another process often lacking within churches) the desired results of incorporating more church members in ministry, most would readily agree the results were minimal at best. Why? The product (spiritual gifts inventories) should have been part of a thorough process that enables people using the product to understand and practically apply the product.

In the process PLACE Ministries endorses (along with many other good organizations and churches), people are given spiritual gifts inventories (product) and then guided in a one-on-one coaching session to determine *HOW* and *WHERE* to best utilize their spiritual gifts in a ministry setting. Many believe that administering the spiritual gifts inventory is where the process stops. This is very wrong—it's like stopping in the middle!

For the process to be successful, churches then need to **equip** believers to utilize their gifts in the ministry best suited for them as **identified** in the spiritual gifts inventory. Next, believers need to be **empowered** (turned loose) to perform what they discovered they were created to do by God with their unique design. The process continues with **encouraging** them to continue fulfilling their God-given ministry. The process is complete when they are trained to **multiply** themselves in helping others discover their purpose and ministry. (2 Timothy 2:2).

Figure 4.1

Do you look for products or processes in turning God's people into ministers? If you incorporate products into your church, without implementing processes, most likely the end results will be minimal and the byproduct will be frustration on behalf of those who attempted to utilize the product. Often, others who attempted to utilize the product and the one who brought the product to the church will all blame the product—when inattention to the process is the true culprit.

Start with the Individual

There is a popular toy for children that allows them to play and also learn to recognize common shapes like triangles, squares, circles, etc. The child is given objects of different shapes and then **encouraged** to place each shape into its corresponding hole of the same shape on the toy box. The concepts of this toy illustrate for churches the importance of people first, programs second. I have used this toy hundreds of times when speaking at conferences and churches to give a visual example of how some churches have inefficiently **connected** members in ministry positions and then how they should correctly **connect** their members into ministry for effectiveness and longevity.

Imagine the toy box as the church and the shapes inside the box as those who have found their place in serving. All too often, people eager to serve try to fit themselves, or someone else tries to fit them, into a ministry (shape on the toy) only to discover they don't fit the ministry responsibility (shape on the toy box). Sometimes, those who get stuck eventually pry themselves out only to return to the back of their church to become comfortable "pew-sitters" who no longer serve in ministries or participate in church activities. Others get stuck and can't get in or get out. They stay in a ministry that is not their place.

After demonstrating this example, I am usually met with laughter because it is all too often true! I then hold up a shape from the toy and say, "With PLACE, our intentional process and tool is about taking the person first (as I hold a shape up in the air), and allowing them to understand how they are uniquely shaped. When a person clearly knows how God has uniquely created them for ministry, he/she fits into their place without any force (as I place the shape easily into the hole it was created for)." After using this visual of the toy, heads go up and down in agreement. My next statement is, "This is easy to demonstrate and agree with, but hard to put into practice in churches." Again, heads immediately go up and down in agreement. Anyone who is involved in staffing a church with workers knows all too much the struggle of having enough workers to fill all the slots.

A church *committed to the individual* will start with the indi-. vidual, not the product, process or program. The acceleration of church programs in the 1970s to '90s created a need for people to carry out these programs. In the 1980s, there was a popular phrase to recruit volunteers for churches. It said, "God is looking for FAT people to serve." FAT stood for: **F**aithful, **A**vailable and **T**each-able. From the '80s to the '90s, the slogan became "every member a minister." Today, this slogan still maintains some appeal.

The slogans and phrases come and go, but have they accomplished their intended result? The answer might be partially, somewhat or for a short period. An unintended result of the slogans, phrases, programs or products might have attributed to the burnout so many church volunteers have experienced.

Sadly, the reaction to burnout in many churches has been the development of a trend to offer relatively few opportunities for church members to serve within their church. This trend has been advocated by many large contemporary churches and new church plants. They recruit only individuals needed for conducting worship services, children's ministries, small groups and maybe some minimal opportunities like mission trips. There are few opportunities to fulfill ministry in the way of organized ministry through the church. Many of these churches emphasize their members doing ministry in their natural flow of life. Sounds good, but is this the way church leaders were instructed to lead their members in the early churches? In Ephesians 4:11-12, the apostle Paul instructs the church leaders to **equip** (train) the members of the church in Ephesus to do ministry.

In reflecting upon this book, hopefully it will become obvious that the reaction so often by church leaders has been to swing a pendulum that goes too far in one direction from one extreme to the other. For example, in relation to church members' involvement and multiple church programs that evolved in the 1970s through the 1990s, the pendulum has swung too far. Today, there is a great deal of pendulum swinging for church members to do very little with regards to member involvement at the local church. Those who have advocated this pendulum swing of having church members commit minimal time to the church have reacted to the lack of excellence many church ministries exemplify because these churches have tried to become all things to all people and in reality have become very little to very few. Also, these church leaders have witnessed the burnout of many church members and their reduced involvement in the local church. Those who advocate minimal commitment witnessed a few committed members having more and more responsibilities dumped on these few.

Churches need to seek balance in their members' involvement, both through the local church and in the communities where their members live, work and play. The answer is not to throw the baby (no substantial ministry led and developed by the church) out with the bath water (processing, determining and eliminating ministries that are ineffective in the church). For churches to balance the pendulum, they must start by focusing on the individual—help them **identify** and understand their ideal ministry and then determine how and where to incorporate them into this ministry with no boundaries. Their ministry may be within the local church, or even outside the walls of their local church, for whatever ministries and opportunities that they are best suited for in Kingdom influence.

Begin with Remember

How can churches help individuals discover HOW and WHERE to serve that goes further than the shotgun approach that is typical in today's church culture? When the words "remember(s)" or "remembered" are typed into a search mode with Bible software, the words appear 233 times in the New International Version of the Bible. The word "examine" appears 36 times in the Bible. It is fascinating to read the verses in their entirety that go along with these words. A few of these references focus on God remembering or being asked to remember His people, both as a group and as individuals. Others refer to God instructing His people to remember Him.

It is often said that if you want to know your future, start with remembering and understanding your past. This same truth applies to church leaders helping God's people **identify** WHERE and HOW to serve in ministry. God's people desiring to serve in ministry should start with remembering, examining and understanding how God has designed them for ministry. Andy Stanley says, **"Self evaluation is** a necessary step in discovering your core competencies" (2003, p. 37).

It is intriguing to realize what God asked people throughout the Bible to remember. He asked the Israelites on numerous occasions (Deuteronomy 15:15, 16:12, 24:18, 24:22) to remember that they were slaves in Egypt (remember life experiences). We need to realize He is asking His people to remember some horrific life experiences they endured.

He also asks them to remember His faithfulness (Joshua 24:3). Part of remembering God's faithfulness is fulfilled when church leaders help their members remember who they are in Christ and understand how God has **equipped** every believer (through the believer's personality, spiritual gifts, abilities, passion and life experiences) to accomplish His purpose for their lives. When God's people can look back at their past, they can realize times when, how, where and with whom God has used them to impact the lives of others. When God's people can realize when, how, where and with whom God is using them currently, they can then begin to process when, how, where and with whom God desires to use them in the future.

Sermons, Relevant Messages and Assessments Are Not Enough

There are myriads of ways for church leaders to help church members understand their past so as to propel them to engage in ministry. Messages that are preached weekly are a major resource to help God's people in this discovery. Messages have a place in helping individuals discern what God is directing His people to be and do. However, if messages were the sole answer, then why aren't there more people who claim to have a personal relationship with God doing more to impact the Kingdom of God? Messages alone, no matter how relevant, are not enough to propel more than 20-25 percent of God's people to engage in meaningful ministry.

Recently, a friend who has transitioned out of vocational ministry into the secular business world wrote me about his new job. He had some interesting comments about what he is experiencing at his new company versus the church environment he worked in for so many years. He stated about his new job, "You don't have to 'be a Christian' to work here, but you are expected to 'act like one.' Interesting change from my decades of working in churches where you were expected to 'be a Christian' on Sundays, but could 'act like the devil' all week long at work."

Whether it is the processes and ways the church is espousing to make a difference in helping Christians develop character or fulfill the ministry of Christ, our current way is NOT WORKING. Someone has aptly said, "Stupid is doing the same thing over and over again and expecting a different result." When are we going to learn that the shotgun approach—putting mass numbers of people in a room who hear the same information and fill in the same note-books—does not in and of itself produce mature disciples in either character or ministry development?

Some church leaders believe the solution is delivering relevant messages, making the message easier to grasp, communicating in a more acceptable method and/or learning the latest fads from well-known contemporary churches. There is nothing wrong with any of this, but these solutions in and of themselves are not working. Yes, Jesus spoke to the masses and had compassion for them, but most would agree that the majority of His time was committed to teaching the Twelve and at times, just one disciple at a time.

Also, there are countless tools and resources developed by ministries like the one I am privileged to lead. These tools and resources that help God's people **identify** elements like personality traits, possible spiritual gifts, abilities, passion areas and life expe-riences are a good starting point. They help God's people begin the process of **identifying** ministries best suited for them, according to their passion and competency. However, they are only a start-ing point. Spiritual gifts assessment inventories are like looking at a skeleton that has no flesh on it. The flesh is added through the teaching that explains what and how elements, like spiritual gifts, can be applied to practical ministry situations. The teaching en-hances the comprehension of the inventories by those taking them. Life is breathed into the flesh (teaching) and bones (personality and spiritual gifts inventories, etc.) when churches help their members process both inventories and teaching through individual coaching.

Ministry Involvement Passion Killers

An entire book could be devoted on how some churches get to such a pathetic state where church members are burned out and looking for avenues to receive and not give their lives away. In a nutshell, our society has become consumer oriented. Many churches have bought into the consumer mentality. Many churches have developed a consumer mentality that requires little commitment by those consumers. Also, let's understand that because we live in a fallen world, there will always be more needs than people to fulfill those needs. Following are just some of the numerous ministry involvement passion killers that have likely lowered the desire for many to serve within churches.

• Passion Killer - Linking Previous Impact to Passion

O O O

Someone or something that has impacted a person in the past may also be the link that disconnects the believer from a desire to serve in the future. We may never know how often someone or something that has impacted a believer's past is the very reason many do not serve within churches. There are four possible previous impact killers.

1. Ministry – A particular ministry that has *favorably* impacted someone's life can often be the link that disconnects their desire to serve. Why? An example might be the ministry of a new members' class. For the sake of illustration, assume that you attend my church and go through the new members' class which starts with the pastor presenting what is involved in having a personal relationship with Christ. After listening to the pastor's simple presentation of what is involved in a personal relationship with Christ, you realize you do not have such a relationship. You then commit to having a personal relationship with Christ. What do you suppose you would think about the new members' class? Most likely, you would have developed a passion for the class and want to **encourage** others to attend.

As the class gains popularity, the pastor realizes the need for administrative help within the class. The pastor would naturally think about you because you have such a passion for this ministry within our church. The pastor recruits you to fulfill the task of administration for the class. You eagerly say yes because of your passion for the ministry. However, to ask you to get a piece of paper from the class to the administration offices of the church is beyond you. You are a people person, not an administrative person. Right *ministry*, wrong *task*—which causes you to lose your passion for ministry and ministry involvement. This happens all the time in churches.

2. Event – An event that has impacted a person's life may be a ministry involvement passion killer. Consider this true story from a young lady who attended my church. She had been inviting her dad to our Christmas pageant for years. Her dad, who was not pursuing a relationship with God, told her no every year. Now, suppose last year her dad agreed to attend and made a decision to radically make his life right with God. What do you think the young lady would think about the pageant event? Most likely, she would be passionate about the event that so impacted her dad.

Suppose this coming year, the Christmas pageant needs greeters. Naturally, they would recruit this young lady because of her passion for the event and she would agree to serving in this task. There is only one problem. She is not a people-person and does not have good social interaction skills because of her shyness. Right *event*, wrong *task*—which causes her to lose her passion for the event and ministry involvement. This also happens all the time.

3. Experience – A previous experience that impacts a person's life may be another ministry involvement passion killer. An example could be someone's experience with the Bible. Suppose a young lady is in a hotel one night, picks up the Bible and begins reading. She realizes she does not have a relationship with God through this experience of reading the Bible. She gets on her knees and commits her life to God as best she knows how to

make this commitment. She returns home and immediately joins a local church where years later she is known as a walking biblical encyclopedia. She was so impacted by her experience in reading the Bible, that over the years she has studied it diligently and passionately. People within the church are continually seeking her out to ask her insight on various biblical passages. Oftentimes she is asked a question that she researches for weeks to help the one with the question on a subject in the Bible.

One year, during recruitment for Bible study teachers, she is recruited to teach a class. There are two problems. To ask her to systematically organize her thoughts and present them in a structured manner is difficult, if not impossible, for her. Secondly, to talk in front of a group of more than two people is a horrifying experience for her. Reluctantly, she says yes, but within a short period has lost her passion for studying the Bible that had previously impacted her so dramatically. Plus, she will probably lose her passion for the behind-the-scenes ministries she is involved in at the church as well.

4. Person – The single greatest passion killer for ministry involvement likely is attributed to another person who has impacted a church member's life. Those responsible for recruiting members for ministry positions have often had previous interaction with church members and positively impacted their life. Examples might include church leaders who have ministered to church members through the death of a loved one, loss of a job, painful divorce, emotional abuse and so on. Those recruiting are not trying to pigeonhole those being recruited. Generally, people go to those they know to fill ministry slots. When someone ministers to another person, obviously a relationship has been established.

One of the greatest passion killers for ministry involvement by another person is often inadvertently created by senior pastors. Some senior pastors create negative feelings through guilt for those

Let me state, and state emphatically, that there is nothing wrong with working toward common goals and a common vision as directed by a pastor. However, when church members are persuaded to leave their personal passion for how and where they desire to be involved in ministry, there is a high probability they will one day opt out of ministry involvement, or if not opting out altogether, will choose minimal involvement which will greatly reduce their impact on the Kingdom.

being recruited. Other pastors kill passion for ministry by convincing those within their churches to work for *their* (senior pastor's) passion as opposed to the member's passion.

How might pastors kill passion for ministry by convincing members to work for the pastor's passion? There are a few superstar pastors who are charismatic, dynamic leaders. However, for every superstar pastor there are a thousand that are not as charismatic and dynamic. The superstar pastors are able to convince their church members to put aside the way church members desire to be involved in ministry. The superstar pastors convince their members to serve where and how they desire church members to be involved.

Let me state, and state emphatically, that there is nothing wrong with working toward common goals and a common vision as directed by a pastor. However, when church members are persuaded to leave their personal passion for how and where they desire to be involved in ministry, there is a high probability they will one day opt out of ministry involvement, or if not opting out altogether, will choose minimal involvement which will greatly reduce their impact on the Kingdom.

Suppose a superstar pastor successfully motivates a church member to abandon their own passion and get actively involved in a ministry hailed by the pastor. Later on, this church member moves to a new area and finds a church where the pastor is not quite the charismatic superstar that the previous pastor was. Remember, the former dynamic pastor was able to motivate the member to abandon his passion for the sake of the pastor's passion and vision. Again, nothing wrong with church members following the vision of the pastor—and it is even right to follow the leadership of a senior pastor. However, if this particular member did not have his *own* passion for ministry fulfilled, he is probably burned out and now is not motivated to engage in ministry at all.

Someone once pointed out that individuals should not be motivated to serve God because of another person. While this is true, it is not the reality. Even people who agree will often spend enormous time using their charismatic skills to winsomely motivate members to serve their ministries and their passions instead of those desired by the member. When that charismatic, dynamic leader is removed, the person is no longer motivated to serve because they have lost their passion for ministry, since *their* passion wasn't realized in the first place. In most cases they blame their lack of ministry involvement on present circumstances. They often do not even recognize they left their passion to fulfill another's (i.e., senior pastor's) passion.

• Passion Killer - Guilt

O O O

Guilt is a passion killer that has been practiced on people to get them to behave and respond to the one inflicting the guilt for thousands of years! We can read of the Israelites using guilt to influence Moses on several occasions when they were not receiving what they believed they deserved from God or Moses (Exodus 14:11-12 and 17:3).

Guilt is a powerful negative motivator that only works for short-term results. Beginning in the 1950s, when churches first started offering programs to reach people, they realized the difficulty in getting members to serve within those programs. One solution had been making members feel guilty if they did not serve. Then and today, this method works only if you are looking for short-term results. In the end, once those made to feel guilty break free from the guilt, there are usually severe negative long-term consequences that negate any short-term successes.

As churches competed for the same members, the treadmill of ministry programming was turned higher and higher. Yes, the previous statement does say "competed" and for "the same members." There is plenty of documentation to show that churches are indeed competing for other churches' members. Research by the Barna Research Group, The Gallup Organization and other entities that compile statistics on church membership and attendance shows clearly that "The Church" in North America is reaching fewer people than in previous decades and the numbers are still declining. Notice it did not state "churches," but "The Church," because whether we like it or not, what one local church does affects other local churches as well. Even for so-called "seeker" churches, we might be shocked to learn how many of their attendees were also affiliated with another church, even if not actively. In earlier days, churches used revivals, Sunday School (small group ministry), special events, etc. to reach those inactive, but not necessarily non-Christians, to grow their church. Today the "seeker" church uses minimal involvement with relevant worship services to reach the inactive. There's nothing wrong with reaching inactive churchgoers, but let's not fool ourselves into thinking The Church is reaching those without Christ and impacting our culture with the gospel.

While interviewing dozens of new members in one particular church over several years, I realized that this church (and this particular church is not alone) was using special events to lure individuals from other churches to ultimately leave their church to join this church. One of my first questions in interviewing members was, "Tell me how you became involved in this church." They would proceed to tell me about a guest speaker or special event that a church member had invited them to or they had seen promoted through the church's advertisements. Without exception, they would say something like, "We could not believe how excellent and uplifting the services and programming were at the church." Let me emphatically state that I am all for excellent and uplifting services and programs in churches, but I am not for stealing sheep from one flock to come and join another flock.

Once churches begin this treadmill of vibrant programs and ministries, they must then recruit volunteers to staff them. Because many churches have tried to become all things to all people, they have had to resort to guilt to keep the treadmill running faster and faster so people will desire to attend.

This true story is told by a church member who had signed up to serve at Vacation Bible School (VBS). During a meeting by the leader of VBS on how to recruit volunteers, the church member asked what to do when they asked someone to serve and the response was "maybe." The VBS leader told the church member to use the statement, "Tell them to pray about it. That gets them every time!" This method may work for a short time, but over the past several decades, this method has left many churches filled with passionless servants and void with those desiring to serve. (As a side note, I am passionate about VBS. My oldest daughter committed her life to Christ one summer at VBS.)

In the United States, the news reporters regularly point out how the federal government is mortgaging the future for our children and grandchildren. I have yet to find a person who does not agree. Many think of the government with disdain because they feel decisions (or putting off difficult decisions) are being made in the short term that are not good for the United States in the long term. In order to appease voters and stay elected, politicians will often sacrifice the safety and success of our future in exchange for the short-term successes of today. Churches have been doing this for decades when it comes to **connecting** members in ministry. We have entered the stage where we are beginning to reap the negative results (fewer and fewer desiring to serve) of placing people in ministry through means of guilt and not passion to serve.

As has already been stated, in many churches, the alternative to removing guilt as a recruiting method for ministry has been to cut the involvement needed by members. The requirements are lowered down to the bare necessities of what absolutely has to be staffed in order for people to participate and continue participating. The biblical response should not be minimal commitment, but instead, proper and healthy teaching on WHY God has a desire for every believer to engage in ministry. There should also be proper teaching on HOW to fulfill God's desire for every believer to engage in ministry.

• Passion Killer - "Other Things" (80/20 Rule)

O O O

The "80/20 Rule" states that 20 percent of the people do 80 percent of the work in a church, but there can be a unique twist when the Rule is applied to God's people serving in churches. The unique twist is where God's people would seek to serve with 80 percent of their time given to their competency and passion for ministry. The other 20 percent would be where there was a need within their church and the person would commit to serve with 20 percent of their time, even if it was not in line with his/her competency or passion. A major passion killer for **connecting** church members to ministry is when members spend the majority of their ministry involvement serving in other areas that are not in line with the church member's personality, spiritual gifts, abilities, passions and direction to ministry through their life experience. Imagine what would happen if church members gave 20 percent of their time serving in other things where they fulfilled the needs of their pastor and church—whether or not it was their "place"—and 80 percent of their time in how and where their passion was fueled? The positive impact could be enormous—both for the member and for the Church!

The 80/20 Rule does not rule out people serving to fill needs within the church, but it helps God's people direct the majority of their time to how and where they are passionate, competent and fulfilled in ministry. In order to help church members live out the 80/20 Rule, church leaders and church members must discover together what the "other things" are that become passion killers for ministry involvement.

• Passion Killer - Over-commitment

O O O

No matter how passionate a person is for ministry and the work of God, they will one day lose their passion for ministry if they over-commit themselves. The passion killer of over-commitment has most likely claimed more ministry servants in churches than most would be willing to admit.

This passion killer of over-commitment is not limited to just those who volunteer their time to ministry, but also to those who are vocational ministers. During the past ten years, I have had the privilege of meeting thousands of vocational ministers, predominately in the United States, but also from countries all around the world. Sadly, I have met many who I have discerned are burned out on ministry because of over-commitment.

If the history of their involvement in ministry were traced back, most likely it would reveal a passion for the work of God, the ministry of God, the people of God and the task of reaching those without God. However, over time, they gave and gave and gave and too often never had those they were serving come alongside and help them fulfill the mission and vision together. Becoming increasingly weary over time, they realized they had nothing left to give, but nowhere to go. They became what I have termed "professional ministers" devoid of all passion for ministry. Encountering these "professional ministers" is disheartening, yet unfortunately, is more prevalent than most would imagine. Church leaders must commit to **identifying** God's people to come alongside their vocational ministers and work together to fulfill God's ministry and vision.

• Passion Killer - Boredom

O O O

The opposite extreme from the passion killer of over-commitment is boredom. Several years ago, George Barna stated in a conference that the American church was losing countless individuals every year because they are not **empowered** to fulfill their leadership abilities in church. This lack of **empowerment** leads to boredom, which leads to non-involvement in ministry.

A true story is told of a man in the early 1980s who had walked away from God and the church in his early 20s, only to commit his life to Christ in his middle 40s. After becoming a Christian, he went back to the small church he grew up in as a child. About a year after rejoining this church, he became a Bible study teacher on Sunday mornings for a small group of adults. One week, he decided to use a short clip from a cassette tape on a sermon he had heard by another preacher. (This was before it became popular to use any technology with presentations.) He made sure the part he was using did not go against the teaching of his church or denomination. He played the clip during his Bible study. After class, the pastor's wife walked up to him and said, "I don't know who you think you are, but you take your little cassette player and don't ever bring it back in here again."

The year was 1982 and that middle-aged man took his little cassette player and all the skills and talents God had given him and proceeded to build one of the largest companies in America, within his industry. Other than his money, that man has given little of his time and talent to his local church over the past 25 years. Tragic, but how often could this story be told in churches all across North America?

• Passion Killer - Incompetence

O O O

Dr. Lawrence Peter, a business consultant, developed a principle in the late 1960s that has been labeled "The Peter Principle." The principle teaches that when people are promoted from their "highest level of competence" to one level above that, they have now hit their "level of *in*competence" (1969). This passion killer is played out over and over again with those who serve within churches. First, a church member is recruited to do one job and they do it with passion and excellence. Next, they're recruited for a more challenging or detailed job and they do both with passion and excellence. After being recruited for a third job, the person is in over their head and no longer does job one or two competently. Before long, they have to relinquish all responsibilities and have now become passionless regarding church involvement.

Church leaders who recruit ministry servants should be committed to matching church members to their ideal ministry. They also have a responsibility to help those recruited have some understanding of where their competence stops and incompetence begins.

The reality is many of these passion killers for ministry involvement could be greatly diminished if churches would earnestly help their members **identify** how God has created them for ministry and then complete the process by **equipping**, **empowering**, **encouraging** and **multiplying** (as explained earlier) . This commitment to the entire process of helping God's people **identify** how God has created them would greatly enhance the long-term service of God's people within church ministries and to ministries outside the church.

Biblical Mandate

Refer to Ephesians 4:12 where Paul instructed the church leaders to "**equip** the saints" (church members) to do the work of the

ministry. Now look at 1 Corinthians 12:7 and Ephesians 4:7—God
revealing that EVERY member of the Body of Christ is gifted to
serve—along with Ephesians 4:12. Clearly, God did not intend
for church leaders to aimlessly let God's people be on their own
in discovering, developing and utilizing their gifts in whatever
ministry they choose. It is time for the Church and its leaders to
fulfill the God-given mandate to **equip** (train, prepare) those under
its care to fulfill ministry as a body to each other, and in the places
God's people live. It is time for the Church and its leaders to fulfill
its God-given mandate to **equip** (train, prepare) God's people
under its care to reach those without Christ. God's people need to
discover how and where to be the hands and feet for representing
Christ within the Church, the community and the world around
them.

"Prove Yourselves Doers of the Word, and Not Merely Hearers" – James 1:22

Some churches will inform potential members up front that if
they have no desire to serve within their church, then they would
be better off to attend a different church. However, upon inspec-
tion in those churches, many who join still do not serve. Yes,
by creating this expectation, they will have a higher percentage
serving, but unless they **intentionally** help members discover
their place in ministry, many will never find their ministry. The
expectation is created that those who join should serve, but the
intentional strategy to help God's people fulfill this expectation is
often missing.

Why do churches make this type of assertive statement and
yet do so little to make it a reality? Some do not know how to go
from "talk" to "walk." Others know how, but are so busy with
other "good" things, that **connecting** every member to ministry is
pushed aside. Others simply talk with no intention of making their
talk match their walk. As has been said elsewhere, this book is

about helping churches and its leaders have their talk match their walk.

Most churches will not make the bold statement that they expect every member to engage in ministry because they have no intention of working diligently to make this happen. No matter how large and apparently successful these churches are today, they will contribute to the loss of influence in the future of Christianity. Most likely, these church leaders, along with myself, will watch this prediction come to fruition from heaven. If I am incorrect in my prediction, then I will need to apologize to them. Church leaders who have the responsibility of involving church members in ministry must ask themselves, "Am I committed to intentionally helping EVERY member within my influence **identify**, develop and implement their passion and competency for ministry involvement?"

IDENTIFYING Evaluation Survey:
For A CHURCH

O O O

To take the evaluations and score yourself, look on the reverse side of the back jacket of this book. You will find a user ID and password. Go to this website: *http://www.mobilyzr.com/ evaluations* and insert your user ID and password. Additional instructions are on the website. Once you are taking the evaluations on the website, the results will be graphed. In this book, you can review the evaluations, but not score yourself or those who take them as a group. Also, there is the opportunity to purchase evaluations and divide them into groups to also assess the effectiveness of various groups within your church or ministry regarding **identifying** God's people for meaningful ministry.

The evaluations are brief and simple, yet the results can be life-changing for you and your church. Invest just a few minutes of time so you can **identify** where you are and what your next steps need to be in **connecting**, **identifying**, **equipping**, **empowering**, **encouraging** and **multiplying** believers for ministry in YOUR church!

O O O

1. My church provides an intentional process to help potential volunteers discover their competency and passion for ministry before **identifying** a ministry position.

    Yes ❑   Some Ministries ❑   No ❑   Not Sure ❑

2. My church has a one-on-one process for helping members understand evaluation tools such as personality, spiritual gifts

assessments, etc. that are utilized for helping **identify** ministry opportunities.

Yes ❑   No ❑   Not Sure ❑

3. My church would graciously support a member who found another church in the area that had a ministry that we did not that was in line with the member's passion group.

Strongly Agree ❑   Agree ❑   Somewhat Agree/Disagree ❑
Disagree ❑   Strongly Disagree ❑   Not Sure ❑

4. My church **encourages** members to **identify** ministries outside the church to be involved with that are in line with the member's passion for ministry.

Strongly Agree ❑   Agree ❑   Somewhat Agree/Disagree ❑
Disagree ❑   Strongly Disagree ❑   Not Sure ❑

5. My church has an evaluation process to determine if members are suited for a ministry task.

Yes ❑   Some Ministries ❑   Few Ministries ❑   No ❑
Not Sure ❑

6. My church utilizes multiple means to advertise and promote ways for members to be involved in ministries throughout the church.

Strongly Agree ❑   Agree ❑   Somewhat Agree/Disagree ❑
Disagree ❑   Strongly Disagree ❑   Not Sure ❑

7. Immediately before, during, and/or after worship services, my church promotes opportunities for members to pursue for ministry.

    Regularly ❑   Often ❑   Sometimes ❑   Rarely ❑
       Never ❑   Not Sure ❑

8. My church **identifies** ministries outside my church for members to be involved in serving.

    Regularly ❑   Often ❑   Sometimes ❑   Rarely ❑
       Never ❑   Not Sure ❑

9. My church highly **encourages** members to **identify** their spiritual gifts before engaging in a ministry.

    Strongly Agree ❑   Agree ❑   Somewhat Agree/Disagree ❑
       Disagree ❑   Strongly Disagree ❑   Not Sure ❑

10. My church highly **encourages** ministry leaders to **identify** members who complement their weaknesses in fulfilling ministry.

    Strongly Agree ❑   Agree ❑   Somewhat Agree/Disagree ❑
       Disagree ❑   Strongly Disagree ❑   Not Sure ❑

11. My church values members **identifying** their passion for ministry and engaging in ministry that fulfills their passion.

    Strongly Agree ❑   Agree ❑   Somewhat Agree/Disagree ❑
       Disagree ❑   Strongly Disagree ❑   Not Sure ❑

12. My church teaches members to **identify** ministries where they can commit to excellence based upon their availability for the ministry.

Strongly Agree ❑   Agree ❑   Somewhat Agree/Disagree ❑
Disagree ❑   Strongly Disagree ❑   Not Sure ❑

IDENTIFYING Evaluation Survey:
For A MINISTRY

O O O

1. My ministry provides an intentional process to help potential volunteers discover their competency and passion for ministry before **identifying** a ministry position.

   Yes ❑   Some Ministries ❑   No ❑   Not Sure ❑

2. My ministry has a one-on-one process for helping members understand evaluation tools such as personality, spiritual gifts assessments, etc. that are utilized for helping **identify** ministry opportunities.

   Yes ❑   No ❑   Not Sure ❑

3. My ministry leader would graciously support a member who found another church in the area that had a ministry that we did not that was in line with the member's passion group.

   Strongly Agree ❑   Agree ❑   Somewhat Agree/Disagree ❑
   Disagree ❑   Strongly Disagree ❑   Not Sure ❑

4. My ministry leader **encourages** members to **identify** ministries outside the church to be involved with that are in line with the member's passion for ministry.

   Strongly Agree ❑   Agree ❑   Somewhat Agree/Disagree ❑
   Disagree ❑   Strongly Disagree ❑   Not Sure ❑

5. My ministry has an evaluation process to determine if members are suited for a ministry task.

Yes ❑   Some Responsibilities ❑   Few Responsibilities ❑
No ❑   Not Sure ❑

6. My ministry utilizes multiple venues to help members **identify** areas to be involved with in my ministry.

Strongly Agree ❑   Agree ❑   Somewhat Agree/Disagree ❑
Disagree ❑   Strongly Disagree ❑   Not Sure ❑

7. Immediately before, during, and/or after worship services, my church promotes opportunities for members to pursue in my ministry.

Regularly ❑   Often ❑   Sometimes ❑   Rarely ❑
Never ❑   Not Sure ❑

8. My ministry **identifies** ministries outside my ministry area for members to be involved in serving.

Regularly ❑   Often ❑   Sometimes ❑   Rarely ❑
Never ❑   Not Sure ❑

9. My ministry highly **encourages** members to **identify** their spiritual gifts before engaging in a ministry.

Strongly Agree ❑   Agree ❑   Somewhat Agree/Disagree ❑
Disagree ❑   Strongly Disagree ❑   Not Sure ❑

10. My ministry highly **encourages** ministry leaders to **identify** members who complement their weaknesses in fulfilling ministry.

Strongly Agree ❑   Agree ❑   Somewhat Agree/Disagree ❑
    Disagree ❑   Strongly Disagree ❑   Not Sure ❑

11. My ministry values members **identifying** their passion for ministry and engaging in ministry that fulfills their passion.

Strongly Agree ❑   Agree ❑   Somewhat Agree/Disagree ❑
    Disagree ❑   Strongly Disagree ❑   Not Sure ❑

12. My ministry teaches members to **identify** ministries where they can commit to excellence based upon their availability for the ministry.

Strongly Agree ❑   Agree ❑   Somewhat Agree/Disagree ❑
    Disagree ❑   Strongly Disagree ❑   Not Sure ❑

Committed to Equipping God's People for Meaningful Ministry

W hat thoughts first come to your mind when you read the title for this chapter? If you are responsible for **equipping** God's people within your church for ministry, do you first imagine thoughts of:

- people you have **equipped**
- people you are currently **equipping**
- people you desire to **equip**
- frustration because of the difficulty of recruiting people to **equip** alongside you
- tools you have used or are using to **equip**
- creative methods to **equip** individuals on your team
- methods or resources you have used that failed miserably
- methods or resources you have used that succeeded enormously
- people you have **equipped** that are flourishing in their ministries

- resources you would like to know of to better **equip** those you are training
- disappointment in individuals you have **equipped**
- ways to create more **equipping** opportunities
- ways to spend less time or shorten the steps involved with **equipping**
- methods and processes to train others to **equip**

Start with the Equipper Not the Equipped

Months before writing one word for this chapter, I reflected for quite some time on the best direction to take. My first thoughts focused on the bullet points above. Almost every day, I had some idea or direction that I felt the chapter should follow so I could logically present the importance of **equipping** and also present ways to help ministry leaders commit to **equipping** those within their ministries.

While I do hope to accomplish this, it dawned on me shortly before starting the chapter that I was beginning with the wrong starting point. This starting point was centered on the *one being* **equipped** and the tools and resources to **equip** the *one being* **equipped**. Just as we saw previously in putting the cart before the horse—training the members before we train the staff—the wrong starting point can drastically impact the process of **connecting** church members to meaningful ministry. For the greatest success and most positive impact, the starting point should be with the one **equipping** and not the *one being* **equipped**.

> *Simply put, the focus and starting point in **equipping** church members for ministry should first be on the **equipper**, not the one being **equipped**.*

Simply put, the focus and starting point in **equipping** church members for ministry should first be on the **equipper**, not the one being **equipped**.

Naturally, the focus has to transition from the **equipper** to the **equipped** if the **equipper** is committed to **equipping** church members for ministry. But, the starting point should focus on what qualifies the **equipper** to **equip**. The following four qualifications of an **equipper** will not be exhaustive in either the number, or the amount of content supplied for each one. Imagine them as the bones of a skeleton that can and hopefully will have meat added through further study on the wealth of resources available to **equippers**.

Four Qualifications of an Equipper

1. **Equipper** Qualifications – Growing Vertically

> [37] *"Jesus replied: 'Love the Lord your God with all your heart and with all your soul and with all your mind.'"*
> (Matthew 22:37)

The **equipper's** qualifications should not come exclusively or primarily from their knowledge, experience or skill at transferring this knowledge and experience to train another person to perform a task. The **equipper's** primary qualifications should come in how intimate the **equipper** is with God. The **equipper** has to be growing vertically in their relationship with God.

The previous paragraph could be copied and pasted from literally hundreds of Christian books written on leading others. What may be different from many other books is to state that what appears to be a spiritually, growing **equipper,** may instead be just a talented, charismatic individual who has learned how to have others follow for various reasons.

The average person may be shocked to know the truth about how many of today's Christian leaders really lack an intimate, daily relationship with God. It has been said that America is about making famous people more famous. This does not exclude Chris-

> *It has never ceased to amaze me how many senior pastors work regularly with their staff and leaders and NEVER have a one-on-one conversation with them about what God is doing in their personal lives. One has to wonder if these senior pastors are growing in their relationship with God.*

tians and its leaders. Oftentimes, Christian leaders have been put on a pedestal, while their followers assume this leader has an intimate relationship with God. Truth be known, they may have nothing more than a great ability to lead and communicate. A Christian leader may be gifted at leading, but not necessarily growing spiritually.

God has and will continue to use individuals in spite of their own personal walks. However, the **equipper** cannot and should not use their fallen nature as an excuse to not grow in relationship with God. It ALWAYS hurts the cause of Christianity when non-believers and immature Christians watch a high-profile Christian leader fall because of sin, or even act in ways that are not becoming of a Christ-follower.

Some of my most cherished memories as a new Christian were with my spiritual father who was the pastor of my hometown church where I committed my life to Christ. Every time we were together in our 18-year friendship until his death in 1994, we would discuss what God was doing in our personal lives. We talked about what God was teaching us in the Bible and through our daily experiences. Not only was this the norm with him, it was typical of the church culture where he was the senior pastor for 18 years. I was shocked when I went to seminary and began to realize that it was not the norm to speak with fellow believers about what God was doing in our personal life. To my dismay, I soon discovered that in most churches, this type of behavior was even looked upon as a bit weird from many church leaders.

It has never ceased to amaze me how many senior pastors work regularly with their staff and leaders and NEVER have a one-on-one conversation with them about what God is doing in their personal lives. One has to wonder if these senior pastors are growing in their relationship with God.

The **equipper** must not only be committed to training how to grow spiritually through a public platform, but also in one-on-one encounters. The **equipper** must be committed to not only transferring knowledge and expertise, but also in teaching through word and action what God is personally doing in their life to transform them into a growing disciple of Jesus Christ. A simple test might be to ask, "With those I am **equipping**, how often do I discuss their personal relationship with Christ and my personal relationship with Christ? What is God currently doing to transform me into a mature follower of Him?" Is God using you to **equip** others because of your relationship with Him or *in spite of* your relationship with Him?

2. **Equipper** Qualifications – Lifelong Learner

[14] "But as for you, continue in what you have learned and have become convinced of, because you know those from whom you learned it, [15] and how from infancy you have known the holy Scriptures, which are able to make you wise for salvation through faith in Christ Jesus." (2 Timothy 3:14–15)

Another qualification that sounds cliché, but is truer today than any time in history is to be a lifelong learner. It has been said that what worked yesterday will not work tomorrow. In today's ever-changing world, we could even state that what worked this morning will not work this afternoon! Maybe that's a bit of an exaggeration, but the point is: the **equipper** must be continuously growing in wisdom and knowledge, both as a person and as an **equipper** of others.

As a member of the Golden Gate Baptist Theological Seminary's council since the mid-1990s and now a trustee at the school, I have heard this phrase countless times: "Becoming a lifelong learner" is one of the keys to effective and impactful ministry. Sadly, for many in positions of **equipping**, this is a phrase often ignored in their ministries.

This morning, I read an e-mail from Jennifer Hembree, a friend and staff member at Eagles Landing First Baptist Church in McDonough, Georgia. A few days ago, I had talked to her just before she was going into a meeting with the senior pastor. She was concerned he was going to downsize and possibly remove some of her current responsibilities. Quite the contrary, her e-mail was informing me of a promotion being offered her by the senior pastor. Previously, they had looked outside the church to fill this position. After interviewing potential candidates, the senior pastor had come to the realization that Jennifer had **equipped** those within her current ministry just as he envisioned **equipping** to be done in many other ministry areas relating to this vacant position. She was shocked when he offered to expand her position and add many more responsibilities.

Jennifer may have been shocked, but my first thought was that she is exactly the person to do what the senior pastor laid out in his offer to her. I have watched her for several years and have been fascinated with her ability to **equip** herself and **equip** those on her team. In almost every conversation, Jennifer shifts to what she can do better and what resources are available to help her better **equip** those within her ministry. Jennifer is a lifelong learner who is impacting others by **equipping** them to do the work of the ministry.

3. **Equipper** Qualifications – Risk Taker

[18]*"But the man who had received the one talent went off, dug a
hole in the ground and hid his master's money."*
(Matthew 25:18)

Yes, a risk taker is a vital qualification for an **equipper** of others. How many stories could be told of investing time and resources into **equipping** an individual for ministry, only to have the individual disappointed by not following through, abandoning the ministry or doing a ministry task poorly?

Shortly after I joined the staff of a church where I would be responsible for **identifying** and **connecting** church members to ministry opportunities, we **identified** a man who wanted to do small maintenance and repairs for single parents and the elderly. Several months after referring him to the senior adult coordinator, I received a call from the coordinator furious about my referral. The church member's schedule had changed and he was no longer able to complete the home repairs the senior adult coordinator was assigning him. From that time on, the senior adult coordinator was soured on me, as well as the process for **connecting** and **identifying** church members to meaningful ministry.

Church members will sometimes disappoint and drop the ball when it comes to fulfilling ministry tasks. However, this does not negate the responsibility to **equip** and **empower** them. Those who **equip** others, but cannot handle the failure of others, will struggle with taking seriously the mandate to **equip** believers for the work of ministry (Ephesians 4:12).

Failure Is Permitted Outside but Not Inside the Church

It is amazing how many church leaders will allow members to fail morally, but will write them off as useless when it comes to their failing in delegated tasks and responsibilities assigned for the church. It is amazing how low the bar is set by many churches when it comes to how their members live life outside the church, yet these members are written off as unworthy of involvement when they drop the ball in a ministry responsibility.

The typical reason for this mentality is that the church unapologetically demands and expects excellence from those involved, as it should. But, maybe we should reevaluate whether excellence is the true motive when it is not demanded by church leaders from church members in their personal lives away from gathering as the Body of Christ. Maybe the motive might be church leaders who recognize what it takes to gratify the leaders' insatiable desire for his/her own success and see people as a means to that end. Aren't we glad we do not have to determine which leaders might fit into this category? If the possible motive for the leaders' success angered you, then maybe you need to evaluate what your motives are in **connecting** members to meaningful ministry.

4. **Equipper** Qualification – Servants

[28]"Just as the Son of Man did not come to be served, but to serve, and to give his life as a ransom for many."
(Matthew 20:28)

[1]"Follow my example, as I follow the example of Christ."
(1 Corinthians 11:1)

The fourth qualification to **equip** others is be a servant. There has been a tidal wave of books and seminars written over the past several years that deal with servant leadership. If you are involved in ministry leadership, most likely you have encountered this tidal wave of information that has swept Christian circles. Countless principles and suggestions have been promoted on what constitutes a servant leader and how to become a servant leader. Below are two more suggestions to add to the tidal wave of information that has flooded those desiring to **equip**.

a.) *Consider how often you do something that is unexpected and might be considered "below you" by those you are leading and equipping.*

Twenty years ago, my pastor and boss was Steve Cloud who was the senior pastor of Northside Baptist Church in West Columbia, South Carolina for twenty years. I remember as if it were yesterday that every time the church had an all-church-clean-up-day (yes, those are mostly a relic of the past), Steve would be the first to arrive and the last to leave. Not only would he show up, he would actually work. The church was large enough that no one would have been surprised if the senior pastor chose not to show up for clean-up. While I did not expect him to participate, he taught me by example what servant leadership entails in practical ways.

I remember much of how he **equipped** me to be a better youth minister by learning how to be a better administrator. Even more than learning administration, I remember vividly what he taught me about being an **equipper**. He set an example by doing tasks (i.e., showing up at church clean-up days) that most would consider menial. As an **equipper** of others, ask yourself **what you have done lately** that others might consider beyond their typical expectation of you (20 years ago when you started the church and did everything doesn't count).

b.) *When was the last time that those you are equipping witnessed you doing something out of your comfort zone?*

In looking at the entire life of Christ, the conclusion is: He left His comfort zone (heaven) to enter mankind's world. **Equippers** should seek to discover their strengths and work to capitalize on those strengths. However, when we are **equipping**, there will and should be times that we leave what is comfortable in order to better **equip** the individuals we are leading.

This past winter on a ski trip, my daughter asked me to do something with her that is totally uncomfortable for me and out of my comfort zone. She asked if next year I would snow ski with her. She said, "All the other dads were on the slopes with their children and I am the only kid skiing without my dad." Do you think I will be on the ski slopes with her next year? Will my motivation be because I just can't wait to jump on the slopes—maybe fall on the slopes—and watch myself get embarrassed as I attempt to ungraciously go down the mountain? Absolutely not! My motivation will be to help my daughter excel at something that is important to her by boldly being with her and not tucked away in my comfort zone. At times, **equippers** must choose to get out of their comfort zones to help those they **equip** to excel in their ministries.

Equipping starts with the **equipper.** Obviously, these four qualifications are only the starting qualifications and are just the foundation for beginning the **equipping** process. Starting with the **equipper**, is like building a house. The foundation is not exciting to look at, but it is the key to the house withstanding the elements that it encounters over time. The **equipper** who is growing in their relationship with God, being a lifelong learner, taking risks with those **equipped** and being a servant has the foundational elements required for being committed to **connecting** believers to ministry.

Missing the Good Old Days

How many times have you heard, "back in the good old days," regarding how something used to be done as it relates to church and ministry? Some church leaders constantly remember how church used to be done. Many relate to the following church member habits from days gone by.

Remember when church members would:

- come to church on Sunday afternoon before the evening worship service for discipleship training

- come on either Sunday afternoon or Wednesday evening for instruction on how to best teach the Bible study lesson for the next week

- take a week of vacation to go to a denominational retreat center to receive **equipping** instruction for their area of ministry

- come to the church on a weeknight to go visit those who had visited the church the previous Sunday

Lowering Involvement Expectations Lessens Opportunities to Equip

There are still some churches that practice some of the previous methods for reaching and **equipping**, but they are becoming fewer and fewer. Recently, I talked to a friend about the lack of **equipping** done by most churches today. He told me, "You're right, but people today are so busy." I do not disagree, but the last time I checked, people today still have the same 168 hours in a week that people 20 years ago had in order to get everything accomplished, including being **equipped** for ministry.

Why does it take more commitment and training to be an assistant soccer coach for a 9-year-old's soccer league than a Bible teacher in a church? An entire volume of books could be written on the following two reasons why churches struggle to **equip** church members for ministry. However, we will only briefly highlight each one.

Two Reasons Why Churches Struggle to Equip

1. Church leaders and church members need to be honest and admit that people have changed their priorities from a life revolving around spiritual matters to one revolving around worldly matters.

This shift in priorities caught on in the mid 1990s and has been gaining momentum ever since. The resulting trend has been to remove as many activities from the church calendar as possible. Naturally, the trend had to be spiritualized so as to justify lowering involvement in church. This first justification claims that church members need to spend more time with their family. However, this claim is not valid—families are replacing family time spent at church with family time in worldly activities. How does attending a soccer match as a family (if the family even attends together) instead of attending church together as a family help them be more of what God would desire for a family? An outside observer could easily come to the conclusion that Christian families have exchanged spiritual activities for worldly activities.

*2. Secondly, we struggle to **equip** by justifying the need for Christians to be involved with non-Christians in the non-Christians' environment.*

On the surface, it appears to be noble to **encourage** Christians to engage non-Christians in their environment, so they should be **encouraged** to do so. However, we have to ask whether this really takes place on a large scale that truly reaches non-Christians more so than in previous days and methods utilized to reach non-Christians? Church leaders are notorious for gathering a few success stories and presenting them as the norm when wanting to change previous paradigms and methods for ministry.

For example, a church cancels Wednesday night activities in order for members to engage non-Christians in their environment. A church member joins a bowling league on Wednesday night. Through conversations on Wednesday nights about Christ, the church member introduces a fellow bowler to Christ. This success story is told to justify canceling normal Wednesday night church activities.

Typically, this type of success story is used to justify that Christians spend too much time together at the church. To be clear, I am NOT opposed to Christians engaging non-Christians in their environments. **We should frequently engage non-Christians in their environment.** What I am opposed to is using only a few success stories like these to justify the elimination of important church activities for the family. I am all for **equipping** church members for ministry. Without devoting time and intentionality to **equipping**, it will not happen on any scale large enough to make a measurable difference.

The old method may have had just as many success stories as the new method. This book is not about the attractional model (inviting non-Christians to come to the church building) versus the missional model (engage non-Christians in their environment). However, the pros and cons can be debated on both sides. Most would agree that if there is not accountability, intentionality and a way to measure something, then the intended results are minimal.

Obviously, we should not conclude that church members should ignore time with their families and only engage lost people on church grounds. The intent is to point out that church leaders have been convinced by charismatic communicators who have built large churches that the bar needs to be lowered to reach people in today's culture. No one would disagree that in today's society, the trend in churches is that the bar has been lowered to reach people regarding commitment, and specifically church commitment.

The problem is with the leaders who lowered the bar. They have convinced others that this is what churches need to do to be culturally relevant. Not only is this a problem, but this misnomer has created churches all over North America that are living with the problem of ill-**equipped** church members. Could this trend to lower commitment possibly be part of the challenge to **equip** church members? Could the leaders of this movement interpret the results as a spike in perceived short-term success, but that will ultimately be followed by disastrous long-term consequences? As a side note, Christ-like transformation is not measured only by how many show up to the worship services of a church and attend a small group where individuals are asked their opinion of a passage of Scripture.

The Church in North America may be sliding down the slope that the Catholic Church in Europe faced at the time of the Protestant Reformation. Without **equipping** church members for meaningful ministry, the gulf between the "professionals" and the members will widen. This gulf will widen unless church leaders will help church members discover their ministry and then **equip** and **empower** them to fulfill their ministry.

Right now, some of you reading this section are disagreeing with these assumptions because your church is reaching people. Please remember that this book is not about what YOUR church, or the big church you look to for direction, is doing to reach people today. It is about what WE (the entire Body of Christ in North America) are doing to reach people. This book is about what future generations will inherit from current leaders to reach and impact the culture for Christ.

Howard Gardner, professor of cognition and education at the Harvard Graduate School of Education, and one of the leading thinkers for our society, hit it dead center not only for society but for church leaders. He said,

"In the interconnected world in which the vast
majority of human beings now live in, it is not
enough to state what each individual or group needs
to survive on its own turf. In the long run, it is not
possible for parts of the world to thrive while others
remained desperately poor and deeply frustrated.
Recalling the words of Benjamin Franklin, 'We
must indeed all hang together, or, most assuredly,
we shall all hang separately.'" (2006, p. 2)

Long before Howard Gardner came to his brilliant conclusion for society, God intended for the Church to be a Body that is
interconnected, instead of each individual local church primarily
looking out for its own interest. When will church leaders come
to the realization that a decision by one church (especially those
large enough to have a platform to influence) impacts many other
churches?

Eventually, Past Equipping Will Dissipate

While writing this chapter, I visited a friend who told me about
the **equipping** (or lack of) within his church. My friend is very
involved in his church. After attending seminary, he decided to
become a successful business leader and serve his church as a lay
member and not as a vocational minister. He was part of a Bible
study class that had grown too large and needed to split and start a
new class. Approximately 15 couples agreed to be a part of a new
class.

This new class went several weeks without a teacher, so my
friend called the staff member in charge of adult education and
offered to teach the class. The adult education pastor did not
call back for two weeks. When he finally did call back stating,
"Sorry it took so long to return the call," my friend had already
been teaching for two weeks! The adult education pastor never

even asked what material he was using to teach. I asked him if the church provided any training for teaching. He said he thought the church was having some kind of training that weekend.

I also asked him what some of the strengths of his church are? He said one is the strong Bible study classes. I asked if my assumption was correct that many of the strong Bible study teachers had taught for 10 or more years within the church and he agreed. He also informed me that in previous years there had been regular meetings for Bible study leaders, but now they were sporadic and leaders generally only communicated during the week of the meeting.

As a side note, my friend was frustrated with the lack of communication in all areas of his church, especially when three full-time ministerial staff had been added in the last year for a total of 25 full-time ministerial staff. He said, "You'd think with that many people they could get around to returning a phone call to a potential Bible study teacher in less than two weeks." What happens in two or three generations when church members are recruited in a haphazard way like my friend and the **equipping** process is all but non-existent?

Even for churches that use almost all their resources to reach the unchurched, there is an interesting insight. The majority of these churches rely on leaders who were brought up in a church culture where **equipping** had equal importance with reaching those outside the church when it comes to disciple-making through teaching. Many churches have been accused of being too inward-focused in areas like teaching. Many younger churches that have become well-known and modeled after seem to be abandoning the model to focus on its members, which includes minimal **equipping** and discipling of its members.

*As with all of life in general, balance is the key. Churches that are older do have a tendency to focus inward, but churches that only focus outward will one day leave a void when its membership is a mile wide and an inch deep. The void will translate to a lack of impact in the culture that can be traced back to not focusing on **equipping** its members.*

Is This the Future of Equipping?

John McArthur tells the following story that illustrates what is happening in churches all across North America. The couple in his story are too often the members leading others within churches.

"...our route took us off the main highways and through some beautiful rural country. We topped one hill, and I noticed near a rustic house a home-made sign advertising hand-sewn quilts. I had hoped to stop somewhere along the way to buy an anniversary gift for my wife. She likes handmade crafts and had been wanting a quilt, so we decided to stop and look.

"We went to the door of the old house and knocked. A friendly woman with a dish towel answered the door. When we told her we were interested in quilts, she swung the door open wide and ushered us in. She showed us into the living room, where she had several quilts on display.

"The television in the corner was on, tuned to a religious broadcast. The woman's husband was lounging in a recliner, half watching the program and half reading a religious magazine. Around the room were piles of religious books, religious literature, and religious videotapes. I recognized one or two of the books—resources from solid evangelical publishers.

"The woman left the room to get some more quilts to show us, so the man put aside his magazine and greeted us. 'I was just catching up on some reading,' he said.

'Are you a believer?' I asked.

'A believer in *what*?' he asked, apparently startled that I would ask.

'A believer in Christ,' I said. 'I noticed your books. Are you a Christian?'

'Well sure,' he said, holding up the magazine he was reading. I recognized it as the publication of a well-known cult. I took a closer look at the stacks of material around the room. There were a few evangelical best sellers, material from several media ministries, a promotional magazine from a leading evangelical seminary, and even some helpful Bible study aids. But mixed in with all that were stacks of *The Watch Tower* magazines published by the Jehovah's Witnesses, a copy of *Dianetics* (the book by Scientology founder L. Ron Hubbard), a Book of Mormon, Mary Baker Eddy's *Science and Health*, some literature from the Franciscan brother, and an incredible array of stuff from nearly every conceivable cult and *–ism*. I watched as he jotted down the address of the television preacher who was at that moment offering some free literature.

'You read from quite an assortment of material,' I observed. 'These all represent different beliefs. Do you accept any one of them?'

'I find there's good in all of it,' he said. 'I read it all and just look for the good.'" (2007, pp. 185–187)

For those who think McArthur's experience is the exception rather than the rule, I would disagree. Even for the so-called teaching churches that invite other church leaders to their churches to learn how they do church, McArthur's experience would not be unusual. Yes, I know that when they invite others to hear how they do church it appears that everything runs smoothly and systems are in place to recruit, train, **empower** and **multiply** their members for ministry. However, when you talk to typical church members in these churches that are honest, you will find that what seems like a well-oiled machine, often is anything but well-oiled when it comes to execution. You will discover competent staff who have thought through recruiting, **equipping**, **empowering**, **encouraging** and **multiplying**, but are too busy figuring ways to market to those outside the church to execute their well-thought-out and articulated plan for **connecting** church members to meaningful ministry.

Challenges to Solutions in Equipping

Writers and speakers who focus only on what problems the Church faces today, without offering solutions, provide some but little value. One of the primary reasons this book has devoted a great deal of time to the problems facing Christianity is because many church leaders and Christians have no clue that the Church is at a crossroads in its ability to impact society. Before we can provide solutions to a problem, we must first acknowledge a problem exists. However, to focus on only the problems, without providing solutions, leaves the Church weak and anemic.

When Jesus came to earth, mankind had a problem and the problem was sin. Jesus was the answer to the problem. His teaching made mankind aware of its problem.

---

*God has always provided solutions to problems. It is no different today, whether for problems an individual faces or for problems facing the Church when it comes to **equipping** her members for meaningful ministry.*

> *To meet the challenges facing* **equipping** *church members for meaningful ministry, those responsible for* **equipping** *will have to have the words "we haven't done it that way before" and "we used to" stricken from their vocabulary.*

The solutions will only come when the problems are acknowledged and then when the solutions are sought from God. He has answers to every problem we encounter— even the challenge to **equip** church members. While this chapter has focused on many of the challenges and realities churches face today in **equipping**, there are also solutions to these realities and challenges.

Many have pointed out that the seven deadly words of the church are, "We haven't done it like that before." Three words could be added to these seven deadly words: "We used to . . . " I have served in three churches working with young single adults in three different states from the east coast to the west coast. Each group told me the same words when I started with them: "We used to have a dynamic group until our core leaders got married." In each situation, they seemed stunned when I suggested we reach others who could become strong leaders for the group.

To meet the challenges facing **equipping** church members for meaningful ministry, those responsible for **equipping** will have to have the words "we haven't done it that way before" and "we used to" stricken from their vocabulary.

Solutions for Equipping

In spite of the disadvantages church leaders face today while leading, there are also many advantages today that past church leaders did not have at their disposal. Following are many solutions that church leaders can and should utilize today in **equipping** church members for meaningful ministry.

• **Equipping** Solution—The Internet

O O O

The Internet has opened up an entire new world to **equip** church members for ministry. Recently, a pastor told me his time in preparing for sermons had been drastically reduced because of all the tools available on the Internet. Because of the Internet, church members today can become experts, from a knowledge and training perspective, in an area of ministry they are interested in learning—and without ever leaving their home. However, we must use the Internet with caution. While its resources are of great value, often ministry must be face-to-face. Also, without face-to-face interaction in **equipping**, the **equipper** cannot observe the character of the one being **equipped**.

My office uses an Internet software tool (www.gotomeeting. com) in working with churches remotely where those being trained can all be looking at the same screen, yet all be in different locations, even different states. As a similar application, have you ever been on the phone with a technical support person who is always asking, "What are you looking at now?" to determine if you are on the right screen for the technical problem being evaluated? This simple Internet software solution allows computer interaction among all trainees, and they do not even have to purchase anything—our office purchases the meeting time and a code is given to each trainee for free access on their part.

This software has allowed my team to immensely cut down their training time with churches. We can train multiple people at the same time from wherever it is convenient for the trainees. Imagine having 10 or more people training from the convenience of each of their own homes by simultaneously looking at the same computer screen being controlled from the trainer's computer in another state or even country. Just 10 years ago, this type of training would have been unthinkable. In days gone by, training like this would have been in a manual, which most of us can't understand, or in person, which would often be infeasible because of the costs associated with on-site training. Today, training by linking remote computers is not only thinkable, it is reality.

• **Equipping** Solution—**Equipping** Experts Abound
O O O

Another solution to **equip** others is to utilize the abundance of experts available to help churches. Individuals, businesses, churches and society in general, today are far more complex than in the past. This discourages many to do nothing but try and maintain. However, with more complexity, there has been a surge in individuals, information and organizations to help churches and its leaders ride the waves of complexity rather than be taken under by them.

You name any subject and there are people and resources available to **equippers** responsible for **equipping** those within the church. Name any ministry area, type it into an Internet search engine and watch how many websites are available. While writing this chapter, I put the words "church assimilation" in my Internet search engine and over 500 sites were listed. The sites included church software tools to help with church assimilation, conferences on assimilation, other churches that provided assimilation resources, relevant articles and training on church assimilation.

As I travel across the United States year after year, it is astounding how many individuals I have met that have developed a strong passion for a group of people or a particular ministry area. I am also astounded by how truly knowledgeable they are. Along with the knowledge, they have acquired an expertise in their passion area or group. Also, it is remarkable how many of these individuals are willing to share their experience, learning and knowledge with complete strangers who have the same passion. These individuals not only desire to **connect**, but also to help others gain expertise and knowledge in the ministry area of their mutual passion.

Several years ago, I was conducting a PLACE workshop in the Dallas/Fort Worth area. At the end of the training, a young man came up to ask a favor. He asked if he could come to Houston the following week where I was conducting another workshop and have dinner with me. He had been a successful businessman for several years and had left the business world to go on staff at his church the previous month. I readily agreed to have dinner with him.

He then asked if I thought the staff member at this church where I was conducting the training—one of the largest churches in the country—that used our material would possibly spend an hour with him answering questions about how they used the PLACE process within this large church. I was sure the staff member would agree, if her schedule permitted. In the past, she had been available to other churches in helping them during the initial stages with PLACE. I called and she enthusiastically agreed to spend time with this new vocational minister. I asked the new vocational minister to be considerate of the staff member's time and try to limit the session to one hour.

When he and I met for dinner, following his meeting with the staff member of this very large church, he told me that at the end of the hour he thanked her for her time. She asked if he had another appointment and he told her he was meeting me for dinner in four hours. She asked if he would like to stay longer. The new vocational minister was floored when this highly successful staff member in one of the largest, most well-known churches in the country spent over three hours with him on how to **connect** members into meaningful ministry!

I have heard similar stories told countless times by those beginning an intentional process to **connect** church members into meaningful ministry by using the tools and resources provided by PLACE Ministries. I have found that PLACE Ministries and these individuals are not unique, but are in scores of churches and ministries across North America that have a desire to help others in their journey to **equip** and train others.

• **Equipping** Solution—Creative **Equipping**

○ ○ ○

At my previous church, the Minister of Education, David Self, provided a weekly tape for the Sunday School teachers. David would teach through the Sunday School lesson for the following week on a cassette. He provided teaching tips and gave insight into the biblical passages. He even used his time on the tape to communicate pertinent information about the church through the lesson. What had typically been reserved for Sunday afternoon or Wednesday in the way of weekly teachers' meetings was being accomplished as David's teachers drove to work, began their day at the breakfast table, ended their night studying their lesson or wherever and whenever it was convenient for each teacher to study.

David later moved to Houston to be the Executive Pastor at Houston's First Baptist Church. This church went almost five years without a pastor. During those five years, David oversaw the education staff, led the entire staff, served as the administration pastor and preached almost every Sunday. This was a daunting responsibility in one of the largest churches in America. One afternoon while in Houston, I popped into David's office to find him still taping his lesson for his Sunday School teachers. David was busy, but not too busy to find time to creatively **equip** the Sunday School teachers who present the Word of God in small and large Bible studies throughout the church. David is serious about his commitment to **equip**. He has found a creative way to fulfill this commitment in a day when it is difficult to gather people onto a church site to **equip**.

Several years ago, I listened to a minister of education gripe and complain that he could not get more than a third of his Sunday School leadership to attend an hour-long workers meeting once a month. Before I offered any creative ideas—like the one I learned from David Self—I asked him if his meeting was a typical workers meeting.

He asked what I meant by "typical." I stated a typical "monthly workers training meeting" in many churches consisted of 45 minutes of the staff member informing the Sunday School leaders (or whatever they are called in your church) what to communicate about up-coming events at the church. Next, the staff member might spend 15 minutes actually training (**equipping**) the leadership. Many churches have 9–10 worker training meetings per year (skipping June, July and December). A committed church member involved in Sunday School leadership (or whatever your church calls these gatherings) might attend 7–9 meetings. This would equate to approximately two hours per year of actual training. He informed me this was typical of his church.

Is it any wonder that he and countless staff/ leaders have difficulty getting church members to attend "**equipping** opportunities" provided by the church? Should church leaders wonder why they cannot get members to engage in ministry when they are so inadequately **equipped**?

A year later, I asked the same minister if he had incorporated any of the creative ideas we discussed into training his leadership. Not to my surprise, he had not done anything but maintain the status quo and continue to complain about his leadership. Churches that take seriously the biblical mandate (Ephesians 4:12) to **equip** God's people will have to find new and creative ways to **equip**.

• **Equipping** Solution—Expanded Ways to **Equip**

O O O

The Internet has recently added several new exciting ways to train. Few churches are utilizing these resources:

• *blogging* – an online journal; for a sample, visit
   http://www.jaymcswainonministryinvolvement.com

• *webinars* – seminars taken online

• *podcasts* – audio and video delivered over the Internet

Modern technology has made these training methods simple to start and they can often be started with minimal or no cost. Simplicity and low cost makes them ideal to utilize for **equipping** those within ministry.

A simple trip to a local bookstore could educate you on everything you needed to get started with a blog, seminar or podcast. Even simpler, an Internet search engine can often do the same. Type each one (blog, webinar and podcast) in the search engine separately and watch the results. More sources than one could imagine are available that give a complete—and free—education on these resources. After educating yourself, gather a creative team (whether in person or through a blog) and brainstorm all the ways blogs, webinars and podcasts could be utilized to **equip** church members to fulfill ministry opportunities in your church.

Recently, while training in the Chicago area, I asked a staff member in his mid-30s how he stays current and relevant in his ministry training. He immediately stated, "Through blogs—I can go from blog to blog and subject to subject and never exhaust the available resources." Interestingly, this staff member had transitioned onto the staff from being a vice-president in a Christian bookstore chain.

Older people sometimes have difficulty embracing anything new, but blogging will become more and more a method that churches can and should incorporate to **equip**. Remember the words, "We haven't done it like that before" must be stricken from our vocabulary to effectively **equip** in today's world. As a side note, many of the concepts developed in this book and within http://www.mobilyzr.com were shaped through **connecting** a team together online (almost like a blog) to read and comment on one another's ideas, suggestions and direction.

Phenomenal Opportunities to Equip

The challenges facing those who have a desire to **equip** church members is great. The opportunities to creatively **equip** today are phenomenal and greater than any time in history. It is imperative to strike the seven deadly words referred to earlier in the chapter that state, "We haven't done it like that before". These seven words cannot be a part of the equation for phenomenal opportunities.

Not only are there countless resources available to **equip**, but the way these resources can be delivered are unlimited. In a time when church members who serve are busier than ever with work, family and activities not pertaining to church, it is imperative to not only **equip** them based on their availability, but on how they desire to be **equipped**.

I Learn Best By . . .

While spending a day with many of the leaders, including the senior pastor, at the United Methodist Church of the Good Shepherd in Lebanon, Pennsylvania, a revealing insight came to fruition that has since been validated time and time again: Church members want to learn and be **equipped** differently.

People learn differently—that isn't new; but, actually asking and hearing from them all the different ways they learn was new. If church members are to be **equipped**, we must consider ways to **equip** based on their schedules, and secondly, we must be willing to **equip** them in ways they learn best.

During a leadership meeting at the Church of the Good Shepherd, the question was asked, "How do you enjoy learning and how do you learn best?" We listed all the ways the 30 leaders in attendance enjoy learning and learn best and they were:

- reading books
- watching instructional videos
- attending seminars and conferences
- brainstorming with fellow team members
- listening to instructional CDs
- listening to books on tape
- visiting and learning from other churches that are effective
- being apprenticed by an effective coach

Next, the leaders ranked their favorite ways to learn from 1 to 8, with 1 being their favorite and 8 being their least favorite. What was more fascinating than hearing how these thirty leaders' best learn and enjoy learning was asking them their least effective and least enjoyable way to learn. Surprisingly, there was more than one individual in every category that determined their *least* favorite way to learn was one of the eight listed as someone else's *most* favorite.

There have been scores of books, seminars, conferences and workshops developed on how to train others utilizing different learning style methods. While unscientifically proven, most individuals who attend trainings to learn how to **equip** others in their particular area of ministry go back into their local churches and **equip** how they best learn or through the easy mode of lecture.

Recently, one of the staff members within our organization attended a conference on **equipping** and reported it was awesome. When asked about the format, she told us they played neat games to teach concepts as they related to **equipping**. While interactive games and role playing utilized her favorite learning style, several of us said we would have been looking for the nearest door to exit at the first break! Although it was an optimum way for her to learn, it would not always **connect** to others. Local churches must begin to learn and incorporate various **equipping** methods for their members.

Know How and Where People Best Learn

Just as important to—if not more important than—knowing how people desire to be **equipped** in face-to-face training is knowing *where* (the environment) people best learn. For example, my least effective environment to learn is at conferences. There are several reasons why I find it difficult to learn at conferences. However, if the conference is recorded on video or audio, I can listen or watch and come away with volumes more of helpful training than if I attended. Quite the opposite, there are others who attend conferences and can focus and get energized on what is being taught because of the energy of the crowd. Still others can read a book, and the words from the page to the person's brain can almost be photographed. Not only do the words and concepts get photographed, but many individuals are even able to pull these concepts and teachings up years later and apply them in practical ways in fulfilling ministry objectives.

Adopting Methods Don't Equate to Adopting Messages

So often in church circles, those who are on the cutting edge are accused of changing both the message and the methods to communicate the gospel. Often, their methods are discarded because the more traditional church leaders do not agree with the message or lack of message that is communicated through these modern methods. Many churches that maintain a sound evangelical theology, along with balanced mission objectives (worship, evangelism, discipleship, fellowship and ministry), become irrelevant in reaching non-Christians and discipling those they have reached because they reject new methods. Eventually, many of these churches begin to slowly die.

In conclusion, churches all over the spectrum—traditional, cutting edge, postmodern, emergent or whatever they term themselves—need to develop ways and methods to **equip** more than just the paid professionals to do meaningful ministry.

EQUIPPING Evaluation Survey:
For A CHURCH

O O O

To take the evaluations and score yourself, look on the reverse side of the back jacket of this book. You will find a user ID and password. Go to this website: *http://www.mobilyzr.com/evaluations* and insert your user ID and password. Additional instructions are on the website. Once you are taking the evaluations on the website, the results will be graphed. In this book, you can review the evaluations, but not score yourself or those who take them as a group. Also, there is the opportunity to purchase evaluations and divide them into groups to also assess the effectiveness of various groups within your church or ministry regarding **equipping** God's people for meaningful ministry.

The evaluations are brief and simple, yet the results can be life-changing for you and your church. Invest just a few minutes of time so you can **identify** where you are and what your next steps need to be in **connecting**, **identifying**, **equipping**, **empowering**, **encouraging** and **multiplying** believers for ministry in YOUR church!

O O O

1. My church provides specific training for anyone entering a
   ministry position.

   Yes ❏   Some Ministries ❏   No ❏   Not Sure ❏

2. My church provides an intentional process to help potential
   volunteers discover their competency and passion for ministry
   before being trained.

   Yes ❏   No ❏   Not Sure ❏

3. My church budget reflects a strong commitment to providing training to **equip** paid staff to lead ministries.

Strongly Agree ❑   Agree ❑   Somewhat Agree/Disagree ❑
Disagree ❑   Strongly Disagree ❑   Not Sure ❑

4. My church budget reflects a strong commitment to **equipping** volunteers.

Strongly Agree ❑   Agree ❑   Somewhat Agree/Disagree ❑
Disagree ❑   Strongly Disagree ❑   Not Sure ❑

5. My church promotes training through the senior pastor's **encouragement**.

Regularly ❑   Often ❑   Sometimes ❑   Rarely ❑
Never ❑   Not Sure ❑

6. My church provides creative training to **equip** those involved in ministry.

Strongly Agree ❑   Agree ❑   Somewhat Agree/Disagree ❑
Disagree ❑   Strongly Disagree ❑   Not Sure ❑

7. My church provides regular training for those involved in ministry.

Strongly Agree ❑   Agree ❑   Somewhat Agree/Disagree ❑
Disagree ❑   Strongly Disagree ❑   Not Sure ❑

8. My church provides specific guidelines on training expectations for ministry involvement.

Yes ❑   No ❑   Not Sure ❑

9. My church provides alternative training for those with non-standard work schedules who are involved in ministry.

Strongly Agree ❑   Agree ❑   Somewhat Agree/Disagree ❑
Disagree ❑   Strongly Disagree ❑   Not Sure ❑

10. My church **encourages** ministry **equipping** outside our church to enhance ministry skills.

Strongly Agree ❑   Agree ❑   Somewhat Agree/Disagree ❑
Disagree ❑   Strongly Disagree ❑   Not Sure ❑

11. My church brings in experts to train in specific ministry tasks.

Regularly ❑   Often ❑   Sometimes ❑   Rarely ❑
Never ❑   Not Sure ❑

12. My church evaluates the effectiveness of training provided to ministry workers.

Strongly Agree ❑   Agree ❑   Somewhat Agree/Disagree ❑
Disagree ❑   Strongly Disagree ❑   Not Sure ❑

13. My church is receptive to evaluating new resources available for training ministry workers.

Strongly Agree ❑   Agree ❑   Somewhat Agree/Disagree ❑
Disagree ❑   Strongly Disagree ❑   Not Sure ❑

EQUIPPING Evaluation Survey:
For A MINISTRY

O O O

1. My ministry leaders provide specific training for anyone entering a ministry position.

   Yes ❏   Some Ministries ❏   No ❏   Not Sure ❏

2. My ministry leader provides an intentional process to help potential volunteers discover their competency and passion for ministry before being trained.

   Yes ❏   No ❏   Not Sure ❏

3. My ministry budget reflects a strong commitment to providing training to **equip** paid staff to lead ministries.

   Strongly Agree ❏   Agree ❏   Somewhat Agree/Disagree ❏
   Disagree ❏   Strongly Disagree ❏   Not Sure ❏

4. My ministry budget reflects a strong commitment to **equipping** volunteers.

   Strongly Agree ❏   Agree ❏   Somewhat Agree/Disagree ❏
   Disagree ❏   Strongly Disagree ❏   Not Sure ❏

5. My church promotes training through the senior pastor's **encouragement**.

   Regularly ❏   Often ❏   Sometimes ❏   Rarely ❏
   Never ❏   Not Sure ❏

6. My ministry leader provides creative training to **equip** those involved in ministry.

Strongly Agree ❑   Agree ❑   Somewhat Agree/Disagree ❑
Disagree ❑   Strongly Disagree ❑   Not Sure ❑

7. My ministry leader provides regular training for those involved in ministry.

Strongly Agree ❑   Agree ❑   Somewhat Agree/Disagree ❑
Disagree ❑   Strongly Disagree ❑   Not Sure ❑

8. My ministry leader provides specific guidelines on training expectations for ministry involvement.

Yes ❑   No ❑   Not Sure ❑

9. My ministry leader provides alternative training for those with non-standard work schedules who are involved in ministry.

Strongly Agree ❑   Agree ❑   Somewhat Agree/Disagree ❑
Disagree ❑   Strongly Disagree ❑   Not Sure ❑

10. My ministry leader **encourages** ministry **equipping** outside our church to enhance ministry skills.

Strongly Agree ❑   Agree ❑   Somewhat Agree/Disagree ❑
Disagree ❑   Strongly Disagree ❑   Not Sure ❑

11. My ministry leader brings in experts to train in specific ministry tasks.

Regularly ❑   Often ❑   Sometimes ❑   Rarely ❑
Never ❑   Not Sure ❑

12. My ministry leader evaluates the effectiveness of training provided to ministry workers.

Strongly Agree ❑   Agree ❑   Somewhat Agree/Disagree ❑
Disagree ❑   Strongly Disagree ❑   Not Sure ❑

13. My ministry leader is receptive to evaluating new resources available for training ministry workers.

Strongly Agree ❑   Agree ❑   Somewhat Agree/Disagree ❑
Disagree ❑   Strongly Disagree ❑   Not Sure ❑

Committed to Empowering God's People for Meaningful Ministry

"I want you to make the same decision I would make 95 percent of the time. We will discuss the 5 percent and work to remove it. Know that I will never belittle you when you make one of those 5 percent decisions."

Those words were taught to me in my twenties when I went to work for my dad. I consider him one of the greatest leaders I have known when it comes to the **empowerment** of others. He built one of the largest residential home building companies in the United States. **Empowering** others is what I consider one of the greatest strengths he used to build the company. Whether pertaining to a business or a church, one of the keys to reaching and growing individuals is to understand **empowerment** and its potential to enhance or limit the individuals within the business, church or organization.

What Is Empowerment?

Empowerment in ministry *is* . . .
- helping God's people **identify** who and what they were created by God to do
- **equipping** and training God's people to do what they were created by God to do
- helping God's people to mobilize and acquire the necessary resources to do what they were created by God to do
- releasing God's people to do what they were created by God to do
- holding God's people accountable for what they have been **identified**, **equipped**, mobilized and released to do in ministry
- **encouraging** God's people to do what they have been **identified**, **equipped**, mobilized and released to do in ministry
- training God's people to **multiply** themselves to help others carrying the gospel forward

Empowerment in ministry *is not* . . .
- hands-off
- abandonment
- control under the guise of coaching
- expecting, but not inspecting
- giving responsibility without authority

Empowering God's people for ministry is like walking a tight rope. If they are pushed too far one way (micro-managing), they fall off the rope. If they are pushed too far the other way (no management), they also fall off the rope (Figure 6.1).

Figure 6.1

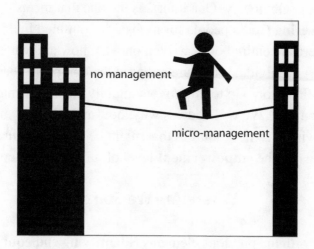

Another way to view micro-management is to view it as a box. Put ministry workers in a box, completely seal the lid and they will suffocate. "No management" of ministry workers is like putting people on a ledge with no safety net and leaving them to either slip or fall from exhaustion.

Thom Rainer describes the idea of **empowerment** in what he calls "The Freedom/Expectation Paradox" in *Breakout Churches* (2005, p. 138).

Figure 6.2
The Freedom/Expectation Paradox

QUADRANT ①	QUADRANT ②
High Expectation/ Low Freedom	High Expectation/ High Freedom
QUADRANT ③	QUADRANT ④
Low Expectation/ Low Freedom	Low Expectation/ High Freedom

Sadly, but not unexpectedly, Quadrant 3 contained the most churches. Obviously, Quadrant 2 is the one that meets the goal for **empowering** God's people for ministry as outlined in this book.

There are entire books written on why, how and when to **empower** individuals that are either in the non-profit sector or the for-profit sector. Go to http://www.mobilyzr.com for many helpful resources. We will address why, how and when to **empower**, along with specific resources that might be invaluable in successfully raising the **empowerment** level of ministry workers within a church.

Where Are We Starting?

As with the previous elements (**identifying** and **equipping**) in **connecting** God's people into meaningful ministry, perception with regard to **empowerment** of believers is often not reality. Without exception, when senior pastors and church staff are asked how many people attend their church, they quickly know the answer. If asked how many are involved in some type of small group ministry, most will quickly know the answer. Almost without exception, the senior pastor, and in most churches, the staff, will know the budget of the church. Almost all pastors, and the majority of those who claim not to count numbers at worship services, actually do know worship attendance. Yet when asked how many serve within the church, the majority can only guess the number serving within their churches. Many will claim a number or percentage, but when pressed on whether they have written data as to the exactness of their claim, it is not backed up with the claim. Furthermore, for the most part, they do not know where their members serve within the church. It does not even register for most churches to know, or even care, where their members are engaged in ministry outside the walls of their church.

Churches desiring to know how effective they are in **empowering** their members for ministry should know where they are starting in the process. Previous chapters have clearly shown the importance of the correct starting point. More than one pastor has made the statement, "We don't count numbers for the sake of numbers, but we count them as a measurement to know how effective we are in reaching others with a compelling message."

---

*The first recommendation I give to churches when deciding to become intentional in **connecting** members to ministry is to discover who and where those already **connected** and **empowered** are serving! I have found that if you don't know where you are starting, you will most likely not know whether you are succeeding or failing in your goal to **connect** and **empower** believers to meaningful ministry!*

As previously stated, one aspect of knowing a starting point is to know who and where your members are involved. Thom Rainer in *Simple Church* (2006, p. 121) states, "For people to take your ministry process seriously, it has to be measured . . . The cliché is true: what gets evaluated, gets done."

He goes on to challenge churches to count numbers horizontally within the church and not just vertically. Counting vertically is only looking at numbers like worship attendance or age-graded attendance without comparing it to other strategic numbers, such as the number involved in small groups and ministry involvement. A church should look at numbers as in the chart below (Figure 6.3) and work to keep each group in balance.

Figure 6.3

Year	Weekly Worship Attendance	Weekly Small Group Attendance	Members Involved in Ministry Within the Church	Members Involved in Ministry Outside the Church
2004	500	350	175	100
2005	560	380	200	110
2006	590	390	215	115

In the chart above, the goal would be to increase small group attendance and member involvement both within the church and outside the church as the worship attendance grows. In order to determine if the goal was being met, the church must know its starting point and track these groups along with their numbers.

In the Ministry Mobilizer (http://www.mobilyzr.com), there is a valuable tool which enables a church to track these vital numbers and evaluate them over time to determine how effectively the church is growing in each category. Whether utilizing the Ministry Mobilizer or not to analyze the numbers, it will be important to move from intuition to reality. When viewing written numbers on paper or a computer screen, seeing the actual numbers can be an eye-opening reality that will both motivate and **encourage** us to **empower** more members in ministry.

Track and Empower Both Within and Outside the Church

During my eighth year in full-time ministry in helping churches **connect** God's people to ministry, I had an incredible realization…

---

*…I came to realize that it was highly unlikely a church had the organizational structure or financial resources to **connect** every member within their church to a ministry within the church. It would not be impossible, but highly unlikely.*

There are several methods for successfully incorporating more believers into ministry. One involves a paradigm shift whereby we must help church members discover ministry both within the church body, as well as *outside* the church walls. There are a growing number of churches that ascribe to their members being involved in ministry outside the church, but never intentionally working to help their members discover what that outside ministry might be. Sadly, if the total impact of those who champion this philosophy could be measured, the results would most likely be dismal, with minimal impact on society and even less on the Kingdom.

It is not an original thought, but "what gets measured, gets results." Ministry must be championed *outside* the church, but church leaders must seek to help those within the church discover what ministry God has called its members to seek outside the church.

Reggie McNeal, author of *The Present Future—Six Tough Questions for the CHURCH* (2003, pp. 67–68) calls this paradigm shift "changing the scorecard." He says,

> "Church scorecards currently reflect member values: how many show up, pay up, and participate in club member activities…
>
> "A missionary church culture will need to begin keeping score on things different from what we measure now. These may include how many ministry initiatives we are establishing in the streets, how many conversations we are having with pre-Christians, how many volunteers we are releasing into local and global mission projects aimed at community transformation, how many congregations are starting to reach different populations, how many congregations use our facilities, … how many hours per week members spend in ministry where they work, go to school, and get mail.
>
> "Until we start making heroes of people who decide to be and act like missionaries, we will fail to turn club members into missionaries. Until we bless people who 'go out from us to reach people who may not come to us,' we will continue to have

> a kingdom vision that is shrink-wrapped to church
> programs and church real estate."

A typical church that has been established for more than two years will most likely have 10 to 30 percent of its active members involved in some type of ongoing ministry within the church. There are exceptions, but these numbers are fairly consistent with my informal research. Countless churches that make an intentional effort to help every member find a place of ministry hit a wall when they realize they do not know how to incorporate a large percentage of them. What started off with great excitement to involve more individuals in ministry within the church, leads to disappointment and frustration, which then leads to abandoning an intentional strategy to **connect** believers in an intentional way to ministry. The key may lie with **empowering** believers *both within and outside* the walls of the church. As Reggie McNeal implies, we may need to change the scorecard.

BUT, We Will Lose Control and Money

Many pastors reading the previous concept of blessing, **equipping**, **empowering** and sending their members outside the walls of their church could not conceive of such an idea. Their fear would be losing control, and more importantly, losing their members' financial contributions to the church.

A pastor within a large church brought this up in a staff retreat. He told them if their desire and plan to **empower** their members outside the walls of the church was successful, it might reduce the financial resources that flowed into the church. The potential loss of financial resources might result in less staff and fewer programs. The staff overwhelmingly agreed that their philosophy was to release their members to fulfill what God created them to do, whether that was within the church walls or outside the church.

This same church had a member who was a top-rated Bible study teacher on Sunday morning. He felt God leading him to buy a hot dog stand and go downtown in his city where tourists and young adults flocked to bars and entertainment establishments. He wanted to find a way to pass out free hotdogs and a soft drink and then let those he encountered know in a winsome way that God loves them.

The pastor's response was, "In God's economy, He will replace our Bible teacher with someone who has been called to that ministry within our church." This same pastor requires each of the ministerial staff (over 20 individuals) to be involved in some type of ministry off the campus of their church. By the way, for the two plus years this idea of **empowering** and blessing members to do ministry away from the church campus has been in effect, it has resulted in record giving by church members to the church.

Recognize Breakdowns in the Intentional Process to Connect Believers

One way to avoid disappointment and frustration is by not abandoning an intentional way to help those within the church **identify** how God has created them for ministry and helping guide them to an optimal ministry. I have consulted with countless churches that start off with a strong commitment to helping their people **identify** a ministry to serve in, only to abandon the intentional process about the end of year two. They start off introducing their leadership to the tool and process that helps believers **identify** their passion and competency for a ministry. It starts with the leadership getting excited about the potential of involving others in ministry, but also desiring others to receive validation in their own journey in how God has, is and desires to use them in the future. Next, they begin building a team to help members discover their competency and passion for a ministry area.

As with any new resource or ministry within a church, there is a certain amount of pent-up demand for those who resonate with the new resource or ministry. This group is excited about the new resource and eagerly endorses it. They become evangelists in spreading the news. However, like any new process, there can be breakdowns. The most common breakdown in the process of **connecting** members to ministry is in the hand-off—when an individual is referred to a ministry, and then the ministry leader does not even acknowledge the individual's desire to serve within his/her ministry. This is the ultimate way of *not* **empowering** believers into ministry—when they are not even acknowledged that they have a desire to serve.

Harry Beckwith and Christine Clifford Beckwith, in *You, Inc.— The Art of Selling Yourself* (2007, pp. 149–151), referred to a study done by a professional association that provided services to over 300 of their clients. The study sought to determine what clients valued most by the association. They expected the clients to list fees and technical skills among the top three. They were shocked when fees and technical skills ranked ninth and eighth, respectively. Number one was for the association to develop long-term relationships with the clients and their company. The second most important value was found to be the most interesting of all … "The speed with which they return my phone calls." (ibid., 150)

> "It turned out that all the callers wanted was for the professional to call back promptly. The callers didn't expect the problem to be solved immediately, and did not assume their questions could be answered quickly. The callers only wanted what almost everyone wants every day . . .
>
> *They wanted to feel important to the other person.*
>
> "People yearn for a quick response because of what it conveys: 'You are important to me.'"
> (ibid., 150–151)

An entire study could be done, and probably should be done, on the negative impact of staff and ministry leaders not responding to church members who make the effort to show their desire to engage in ministry, but are not even given the courtesy of someone acknowledging their desire.

Here's a perfect example of what can happen. This story involves one of the sharpest couples I have met in a long time. They have been **empowered** by their current church staff to implement and oversee the process of **connecting** members to ministry within their church. For over 10 years, the woman was the administrative assistant for the head of a leading Christian ministry that has impacted millions of believers and non-believers. Before retiring and moving to the city of their current church, they had joined a church in another city and willingly responded to a staff member's plea to the church members to get involved. After responding to the plea, they were never contacted. Finally, after a couple of months, they contacted the staff member who had never contacted them. Surprisingly, they were politely informed that the church did not need any help.

This couple did not believe in "church-hopping," but after two years they asked themselves, "Why are we going where we are obviously not needed." They left that church and joined a church almost across the street. Within a few weeks after joining, they engaged in ministry where they spent many years serving within their church. Sadly, this couple's experience in the church that never responded or even acknowledged the couples' desire to engage in ministry could be told over and over again in churches.

From Jobs to Tasks/Responsibilities

Empowering more people in ministry can also be done by taking existing jobs and breaking them down into tasks and responsibilities that can be assigned to others. When churches and ministry leaders help individuals **identify** their competency and passion for ministry, leaders can then break down their jobs into specific tasks that can be delegated or shared with others who also have competency and passion for these tasks and responsibilities. The current involvement of members could be dramatically increased simply by having ministry leaders break down their current jobs into tasks and responsibilities and delegating them to others.

For example, someone who teaches a Bible study could enlist others to help research relevant material that would make the Bible study teacher even more effective in impacting others through teaching the Bible. (See Figure 6.4)

Figure 6.4

NAME	POSITION	TASK/ RESPONSIBILITY	INDIVIDUAL(S) EMPOWERED
John Doe	Small Group Leader	• Research small group curriculum	Jay McSwain
		• Prepare teaching exercises	Sally Jones
		• Nurture small group	Ginger McSwain
		• Organize fellowships/ socials	Barbara Wheeler
		Organize ministry opportunities for small group	John Smith
		Outreach to potential members for small group	Jane Doe
		Numerous details (report to church those attending, communicate to group church desires, etc.)	Paul Jones

Imagine what would happen if every ministry leader within a church made it his/her goal to release tasks/responsibilities they currently do to those within their ministry! Imagine not only more fulfilled individuals who now have meaning in their lives, but the expanded reach of those individuals to those who need the life-changing message of the gospel.

Because of my ministry, I am often away from my local church on Sunday. My Bible study teacher and I were talking one Friday night when I was away from home working with a church. We discussed my hectic schedule and how much I missed being a part of the class. I told him he did an incredible job helping me stay **connected** to the class through his phone calls and personal **encouragement**, but at times I still felt disconnected. It is only natural when we miss a few weeks to feel disconnected.

> *Imagine what would happen if every ministry leader within a church made it his/her goal to release tasks/responsibilities they currently do to those within their ministry!*

As we continued to talk, we discussed his work schedule, its demands and how he was not being able to give proper time to preparing to teach the Bible each week at church. We decided how valuable it would be for him to develop a team to help him research, investigate and prepare his Bible study for the class. I agreed to be his first volunteer to study the lesson with him and pass along whatever nuggets I found that would support his teaching. He told the class about our conversation and three other members volunteered to be a part of his preparation team. Another member agreed to set up a website where we could share information with each other throughout the study.

A few months later, I was with one of the couples from the class. They told me about a neat exercise our teacher did with the group the Sunday before (when I was on the road at another church). He took a passage of Scripture, divided the class into pairs—prayer partners—and asked each member to share a specific prayer request with their new prayer partner. He asked that each person pray that Scripture for their partner's specific request throughout the week, and then give an update the following week to their prayer partner. The idea was one that I had given him weeks earlier for the passage he was teaching on that involved prayer. I was beaming with excitement as the couple told me about the impact of this exercise on their lives. Since then, my teacher has used my input, along with the team's, on numerous occasions.

By dividing the tasks and responsibilities, we increased those involved in teaching and helped someone like me feel more **connected**. Four new people now contribute in teaching the class alongside our Bible study teacher. Again, the point is not to just make more people busy, but to provide meaning to those **connected** and thus impact those members both within and outside the church.

Think Creatively

Some pastors enlist a creative team to help in communicating the message and other aspects within a worship service. Why can't a church enlist multiple people to fulfill certain tasks in most ministry areas like teaching the Bible in small groups or Bible study? At times, ministry leaders naturally give away tasks because of necessity. How much more impact could churches have if ministry leaders would approach **empowerment** from an intentional perspective?

Conclusion—
10 Compelling Reasons for Empowering Others

1. Biblical

O O O

Ephesians 4:12 tells leaders to **equip** other believers "for the work of the ministry," not for the sake of **equipping**, but for the sake of **empowering** others for a purpose. Every church should have as its goal to both **equip** and **empower** every person who affiliates themselves with that body of believers. Books, seminars, conferences and consultants have been developed on how to grow a church, how to have a healthy church, how to develop a seeker-friendly environment, how to have a mission church and so on. Why not consider building a biblical church where one of the core foundations would be to **empower** believers to be and do what God created them for while on earth? The most compelling reason to quit giving lip service to **empowerment** or articulating and rationalizing why the church should not **equip** and **empower** every member is—it is a biblical mandate to fulfill the role of **empowerment** as a church.

1 Peter 4:10 teaches every believer to "use whatever gift he has received to serve others." God did not intend for the clergy to be the only participants in ministry. He **equipped** every believer to minister within His Body. The New Testament teaches that all believers are priests. Priests enter the presence of God and serve His people on His behalf.

James 1:22 teaches believers to practice Christianity, not just be a Christian. Too many Christians think and act as if we can choose either "to be" or "to do" in God's family. It is not an either/or choice, but a both/and command. Churches that do not **empower** believers to be involved are indirectly contributing to those believers' disobedience of God's directive for their lives.

The parable Jesus told in Matthew 25:14–30 is an indictment for a believer not using the talent God gave him/her to fulfill their purpose. Jesus had harsh words for the person who takes what God gives them and does not use it to make a difference in the Kingdom.

What would have happened if the priests appointed to go before God during Old Testament times had chosen not to fulfill their responsibility? Far too often, Christians look at the mercy and grace of God, while ignoring His wrath. When a church fails to **empower** its members to fulfill their priestly responsibilities, it may have God's hand removed from that church, and it may even experience His wrath. What if Jesus had decided not to be our priest before the Father? An eternity apart from God would have existed for all mankind. Churches, along with individual believers, will be held accountable for the eternal destiny of those without Christ.

2. Two Are Better Than One

O   O   O

Ecclesiastes 4:9—"Two are better than one, because they have a good return for their work." Good common sense, which God reveals in Scripture, points to **empowerment** because of the impact that involving others can have on the Kingdom. While our society promotes individualism, this was never God's plan for a believer's life. The beauty of **empowering** others is that when one falls down, the other is there to pick them up. Churches that inject this **empowerment** principle into their spiritual structure are building a structure that will stand strong and be in line with God's directive for His priesthood.

After moving back to Atlanta several years ago, I became very involved in helping believers in my church get **connected** to ministry. At the end of the first year, I came to three conclusions:

i. The greatest asset my church had in getting believers **connected** into ministry was me.

ii. The greatest liability in getting believers **connected** into ministry was me.

iii. If we wanted to have greater results in **connecting** believers to ministry, we needed people whose strengths complemented my weaknesses—like organizing, managing and perfecting the processes and systems we were utilizing to **connect** believers to ministry.

Today, I am not the greatest asset my church has in **connecting** believers to ministry. The team now assembled is the greatest asset. In building the team, we **empowered** others to do what I was attempting to do inadequately, or at times not attempting at all, which let details slip through the cracks. The team filled the gaps of my individual weaknesses and greatly increased the effectiveness of my leadership, and thus our overall success in **connecting** believers to ministry.

3. Fluidity of Peoples' Lives

O O O

Recall the phrase, "One expectation you can have is nothing is constant and change is certain." While most think of this as a modern-day phrase, it is actually a biblical concept given thousands of years ago by God in Proverbs 16:9 which states, "In his heart a man plans his course, but the Lord determines his steps." People who oversee and are involved in ministries within a church will flow in and out of those ministries based upon the circumstances of their lives. We live in a fluid society today.

Yes, ministry direction and vision will change as the makeup of those who are part of a church change. A new pastor, or a change in staff and ministry leaders, will result in changes in vision and direction. However, it is a given that to have long-lasting

impact, there has to be some continuity over a long period of time
in existing ministry focus and direction. The constant changing
of people who fulfill ministry roles in a church is a vital reason to
empower as many of God's people as possible within a church.

Veteran church leaders for years have brought up that in years
gone by, churches would continue to operate a ministry or program
long after its effectiveness had diminished. I would agree, but
point out that in many situations these ministries or programs *could*
still be effective and have impact through that church. What happens more times than we desire to admit is that only a few people
are involved in the ministry or program. As the lives of those
few change—not as much time to devote to the ministry, burnout
within the ministry, move to another city, etc.—there are fewer and
fewer people to assume the responsibilities and perform the tasks
that made the ministry or program so effective in its early stages.

As the team dwindles, the remaining team members often take
upon themselves the responsibilities and tasks of departed team
members. The existing team is sometimes inadequate to fulfill
these responsibilities and tasks. Secondly, they may not have suffi-
cient time to carry out the ministry or program goals as effectively
as they did when there was a full complement of team members
carrying the load. These inadequacies lead to frustration and burnout and often the abandonment of a ministry or program that had
not fulfilled its usefulness within the church or community.

Ministries should not be carried on when there are inadequate
people resources to fulfill them. However, in most cases there
would, could and should be an alternative. The alternative would
be to continually recruit and **empower** others to *constantly* come
alongside existing team members. Churches in today's fluid society should expect and plan for people to flow in and out of ministry
involvement. If churches would seek to intentionally **identify**,
equip and **empower** every person within the church, then many
ministries and programs that are abandoned for the wrong reasons
could still flourish and impact many for the Kingdom.

4. Future

○ ○ ○

If one thousand pastors and church leaders were surveyed and asked if they valued the future of their church, most likely 100% would say yes. If these same pastors and church leaders were observed staffing ministries, most likely there would appear to be a contradiction.

This contradiction can be explained in a familiar example regarding the federal government and its handling of the future. Citizens are outraged that the federal government is continually mortgaging the future of our children and grandchildren to fund and pay for debts today. The majority of churches are no different. So few people are **empowered** to do ministry that these few work until they are burned out. They often become consumers with the mentality that the church owes it to them to now meet their needs. The culture of church has done this for so long now that it is difficult to have adequate people to staff the ministries of the church.

The solution proposed by many leading-edge churches is to remove ministries previously administered by the church. Leaders then **encourage** church members to now use that time to spend with their family and just do ministry as they go about their daily lives with the people they encounter.

I don't argue that more time should be spent as a family and that ministry needs to also be performed outside the walls of the church. However, I contend that the time previously committed to church ministry simply gets filled up with people going and doing "stuff" that will not make one ounce of difference as to where others will spend eternity. I also contend that not much ministry takes place unless the church leaders teach their members how to **identify** their competency and passion for what God has called them to do in ministry. Beginning at the point of **identification** of a specific ministry, the church should wholeheartedly **equip** and **empower** their members for what God has called them to do, whether it is under the direct influence of the church or in ministry outside the walls of the church.

The future of the church and its individual ministries would be much brighter if church leadership would take seriously the mandate to **equip** and **empower** *every* member. If churches would make the effort to continually **empower** the majority, rather than settling for the few, the current trend to eliminate weakened ministries would no longer be necessary, since ministries would remain strong and effective.

5. Necessary for Believers in Obedience to Christ

Jesus teaches in Matthew 25:14–30 that believers will be held accountable for using their gifts. There will be a harsh judgment for those who do not use their gifts for Kingdom work. Those who oversee the spiritual well-being of other believers must **empower** those believers to discover, develop and deploy their gifts in ministry. Churches can develop different ways for God's people to discover their gifts, but if they do not help to **empower** those they oversee, believers will likely not live out what they discovered about their ministries and spiritual gifts.

As has been previously noted, the Old Testament refers to priests that went before God for the people of God. What if God had told them to present sacrifices on behalf of the people, but then He would not allow them to offer the sacrifices? This sounds ludicrous to those of us who look back in history at God's calling of priests and what He asked them to do on behalf of His people. How often do pastors and church leaders tell their people to get involved, only to then be the gatekeepers that prevent their people from being **empowered** to do what they, and more importantly God, mandates them to do?

6. Complex Issues Require **Empowered** Specialists

○ ○ ○

Society today is far more complex and faster paced than any time in history. This trend is not going to change. Along with this complexity has come a tremendous increase in issues the Church must address if it is to continue influencing Christians and convincing non-Christians that Christ is the answer for all mankind.

These complex issues do not catch God by surprise, and He has already **equipped** His Body to deal with them.

In previous times, it has been enough to let the "vocational/professional minister" be the specialist in the issues people faced. This was never God's intention, but just how it has been.

The problem is "vocational/professional ministers" can no longer be looked upon as specialists because there are now so many issues people encounter in day-to-day living. God called all believers into the priesthood to be **empowered** to deal with these complex issues. Many church members have become **equipped** on their own to be specialists in dealing with many of these complex issues.

George Barna refers to the need to develop teams in the same fashion as I am discussing compelling reasons to **empower** every church member. He states, "Great leaders solve problems creatively, enabling them to overcome a broader range of problems and to devise lasting solutions to vexing problems." (2001, p. 79) Having more people **empowered** will enable churches to meet the challenges faced by the complexity of our society and to develop the specialization needed to meet those challenges. To expect a few "professionals" to meet that specialization is no longer realistic. It may have been good enough in previous years to have a few (vocational/professional ministers) know a little about a lot to reach the many. Today, many (all who attend a church) must know a lot about a little to reach the many. **Empowerment** is a key to this specialization needed to reach and keep others within a church.

7. Creates Loyalty

○ ○ ○

In the May, 2005 issue of the *Harvard Management Update*, there was an article entitled "The New Loyalty: Make It Work for Your Company" by Lauren Keller Johnson. The article focused on loyalty between employers and employees. Johnson suggested how to increase loyalty between both employers and employees. She states,

> "Jobs that provide variety and the freedom to make decisions and mistakes engender extensive loyalty, the experts note. Allowing people to take owner- ship of projects gives them the opportunity to de- velop new skills and, just as important, the chance to show what they can do." (ibid., 3)

Empowering church members to fulfill their God-given purpose creates loyalty through fulfillment and the opportunity to make a difference in the lives of others. While some churches brag about their church being a beginning point for believers with the next stop being a more mature church, most would agree this is not the way to impact society long term. Being an inch deep and a mile wide may be good for "numbers" and what most today equate with "success," but it is not healthy for the long-term sustainabil- ity of either the local church or the Church at large. **Empower- ing** church members to do ministry will create loyalty which will equate to stability and thus to the long-term health of the local church and the Church.

8. Numerical Growth

O O O

The passage in Matthew 9:37–38 is likely familiar to many of you reading this book. Jesus says, "The harvest is plentiful but the workers are few. Ask the Lord of the harvest, therefore to send out workers into his harvest field." Most pastors who teach on these verses use them to exhort more people to get involved in ministry so more people will become Christians. It seems so practical that the more Christians that are **identified**, **equipped** and **empowered** for ministry, the more people who will enter into a personal relationship with Christ. Not only is it practical, but it is true—provided the ministry and those involved in being **empowered** do not lose focus on the purpose for serving others.

Empowering others to fulfill ministry with the proper focus will result in more people being introduced to a relationship with Christ!

While the majority will agree with this in theory, they do so little to make it a reality. Why? I have a theory as to why there are so few workers to impact those who are introduced to a personal relationship with the Savior through many ministries within a church.

There has been a tension, and rightfully so, between those who have been labeled proponents of the "social gospel" versus those labeled "Bible thumpers" who are only interested in others accepting Jesus as their Savior. The criticism of those who are interested in the social gospel is that they will generously work to provide food and water for those disadvantaged, but never mention the Living Water and Bread of Life that nourishes one's soul both now and throughout eternity. The criticism of those only interested in introducing others to Christ as Savior is that this group often ignores

> *Empowering others to fulfill ministry with the proper focus will result in more people being introduced to a relationship with Christ!*

passages like Matthew 15:32—where Jesus had compassion for those who were hungry and acted upon His compassion by feeding the four thousand who had gathered to hear Him.

The effectiveness of *both* groups is diminished when extremes are practiced by either group. **Empowering** believers to be the hands and feet of Jesus, while helping them stay focused on their mission as His ambassadors to introduce others to Jesus, will result in increased growth, not only in local churches, but in eternity.

9. Lowers Conflict

How many problems and how much conflict in churches could be done away with if more people were **empowered** in ministry?

One of the single greatest ways to reduce conflict and negative feelings and actions in churches is to **empower** *more people.*

Many people become negative and critical when they are doing too much. They feel used by others and experience burnout, even if they don't feel used. The reason this often happens is that not enough people are **empowered** to carry out the ministry.

On the other side are individuals doing nothing or contributing minimally to the church's goals and vision. Most likely, you have noticed those on this side often throw stones at those who are doing everything. How many times have you witnessed people sitting at a sporting event criticizing the players who are competing with every ounce of energy they have, yet only to hear boos from those in the stands? The same can be witnessed from many of those who sit on the sidelines with regard to ministry involvement. Yes, some are just plain "mean-spirited," but many want to become engaged and have simply never been given the opportunity, so they just criticize and create conflict.

Some of you are part of, or know of, churches that have few opportunities to serve compared to the number who attend weekly services or ministries within a church. They might point out that there is minimal conflict at the church and come to the conclusion that one of the keys to limiting conflict is in asking for small commitments from a small percentage of members and attendees. Others of you are part of, or know of, churches that seem to always be promoting involvement and then seem to be in constant conflict yielding many unhappy members and attendees.

> **Empowered** *servants often resolve their own complaints which reduces conflict.*

What may be happening is that the first church is under-committing and over-delivering to those who desire to serve while the second church is over-committing and under-delivering. Which church would you want to attend? The majority would choose the first church because there is less conflict due to the under-committing and over-delivering of expectations. While there may be little conflict, the first church's long-term impact will be minimal.

Is there a middle ground? Yes! Design an intentional strategy for **connecting** believers to ministry and work to **empower** every person that has a desire to be **empowered**. These **empowered** servants will use their energy that previously created conflict to now reach others through their ministry involvement. An interesting question to be answered in heaven is whether the Grecian Jews, who were complaining "against the Hebraic Jews because their widows were overlooked in the daily distribution of food" (Acts 6:1) were part of the solution to their problem. Don't be surprised if the ones complaining were part of the solution!

Empowered servants often resolve their own complaints which reduces conflict.

10. Increased Financial Support

O   O   O

We can dance around the issue all we want, but it takes financial resources to operate ministries that churches provide to their members and their communities. If churches want to reach those who don't have a relationship with Christ, it will need financial resources. If churches want to fund ministries, they must **empower** members to fulfill ministry. George Barna says his research "confirmed a powerful link between giving money and giving time to the church . . ."

> "We discovered that often people donate time and energy first, then make serious financial commitments to the church later . . . People who become active participants through teaching, serving as lay leaders, participating in a small group, leading a Sunday School class, volunteering to help or participating in a 12-step group through the church are about 50 percent more likely to donate funds to the church than are people who are not involved in any of those ways." (1997, p. 50)

Most para-church ministries understand the concept of money and involvement. It is the reason many of them are constantly looking for individuals with financial wealth—if they become a working member of their board, then they become financial contributors to the ministry.

My dad led my family's homebuilding business many years ago to commit 10 percent of the profit to fund worthy causes of which most are related to Christian ministries. Several years ago, we determined that even with the opportunity to give away substantial sums of money each year, we could not possibly fund all the requests we received through our foundation. Many foundations have complicated requirements for what they fund. My family foundation, The MDC Today Family Foundation, has simple criteria that supports the reason churches should **empower** their members and regular attendees for ministry. The main criteria for our foundation is that either a family member or an employee of our business have to be involved in the organization we fund. We do not look for opportunities to sit on a board of directors for an organization. Instead, we look for opportunities to provide financial support where we can engage more directly in working alongside the organizations we support to help them fulfill their mission.

If churches would only spend more of their resources in **empowering** God's people in ministry involvement, then the senior leadership could do away with using guilt and "beating people up" to solicit funds. It does not take a sophisticated research organization like The Barna Research Group to understand the truth in the words of Jesus. He said, "For where your treasure is, there your heart will be also." (Matthew 6:21) Jesus did not have to form a research company to know that **empowered** servants willingly give their financial resources to impact the Kingdom!

A Tragic Story of Control and Pride

The following is a true story. The names have been changed to protect the guilty! Bill, a member of Trinity Church, had been working on incorporating a new ministry within his church. He visited other churches and started reading and studying the impact this ministry had in churches all over the world. He had put more time in strategizing, planning and beginning this ministry over the past year than he had put in his job. He was working through a staff member at the church and had the blessing of the senior pastor. The entire church believed this ministry was vital to the power the church would have in impacting lives both within the church and the community. Bill recruited a core team that met at least weekly to brainstorm the best way to incorporate this ministry within the church. The team took on Bill's enthusiasm. They began the process of learning the principles that were vital to this ministry's success. Included in each meeting was the staff member that was the liaison between the team and the staff.

Bill and the ministry team had many members involved in the ministry. The team began to get excited as they watched the ministry impact countless individuals, both directly and indirectly. Bill regularly gave a status report to the staff member and the senior pastor on the ministry. He kept them informed on the details of all events that were taking place in which this ministry was involved—both in the church and in the community.

At some point, there came an event in which the senior pastor had participated in for years. Bill was asked to participate in the event, along with the senior pastor. Bill, not the senior pastor, was invited to take the lead in opening the event. Bill is not a power-hungry type of individual. He was just thrilled that the ministry was being invited by another ministry within the church to work together to impact literally thousands of lives. Somewhat naïve to power struggles and egos that go on in churches and often the lives of leaders, Bill opened the event. This turned out to be a bad decision on Bill's part.

You would think the senior pastor would be elated that one of his church members had stepped up and taken such an active role in starting the ministry that was beginning to impact so many lives. Sadly, this was not the reaction of the pastor. The pastor let his pride and controlling nature take over. He called the staff member that was the liaison to Bill and his team in and "read him the riot act." He informed the staff member that Bill had taken away his role in the event that he had done for years. Furthermore, he wanted Bill stripped of the leadership role for the ministry and this role given to the staff member instead. The pastor wanted the staff member to run all future details through him before executing details and events in this ministry.

Tragically, this true story of control and pride could be told about churches all over the world. Churches and pastors often talk about **empowering** members for ministry. However, their own insecurities, pride and control often put up a wall that unsuspecting members run straight into when attempting to fulfill their God-given purpose within a local church. Yet, at the same time, these pastors and churches will teach convincingly that the Bible and God call believers to serve within the local church.

Recently my four-year-old daughter was showing off at church to some teenagers. She was jumping around and singing a song. She suddenly turned around without watching where she was going and ran straight into a wall. She immediately began crying and a large knot formed on her forehead. My guess is she will not run into that wall again!

How many church members are running into walls of pride and control from pastors and church leaders who regularly are telling them to get involved in church?

When they do, they run into walls in implementing their God-given call by these same pastors and church leaders. Gomer Pyle, that great philosopher, often quoted an old proverb, "Fool me once, shame on you; fool me twice, shame on me."

It may be shocking how many church members have encountered pastors like Bill's. On second thought, maybe it is not so shocking for those who study the church from the perspective of **empowering** believers to fulfill their God-given purpose through service in their local church. Some would say the church needs better communicators or more tools and resources to help people get involved in ministry. But, maybe the church needs pastors, church staff and ministry leaders to stop and think about what they are *really* teaching regarding members involved in ministry. They should think and evaluate whether they are *truly* **empowering** members to engage in ministry. Unfortunately, many pastors, church staff and ministry leaders need to repent of their pride and control issues that not only stifle their churches and its members, but also their own relationship with God.

I wish Bill's story had a happy ending. As of this writing, Bill is walking around crying with a big knot on his head as it relates to his involvement with the ministry he is so passionate about in his church. While I hope Bill does not walk into that same wall again, more importantly, I hope Bill and his pastor find a way to break down the wall altogether. Bill has been receiving Godly advice on how to resolve this impasse with his pastor. For the sake of the Kingdom, Bill's church and his own calling, let's hope God is ultimately glorified in this matter of **empowerment**.

EMPOWERING Evaluation Survey:
For A CHURCH

O O O

To take the evaluations and score yourself, look on the reverse side of the back jacket of this book. You will find a user ID and password. Go to this website: *http://www.mobilyzr.com/ evaluations* and insert your user ID and password. Additional instructions are on the website. Once you are taking the evaluations on the website, the results will be graphed. In this book, you can review the evaluations, but not score yourself or those who take them as a group. Also, there is the opportunity to purchase evaluations and divide them into groups to also assess the effectiveness of various groups within your church or ministry regarding **empowering** God's people for meaningful ministry.

The evaluations are brief and simple, yet the results can be life-changing for you and your church. Invest just a few minutes of time so you can **identify** where you are and what your next steps need to be in **connecting**, **identifying**, **equipping**, **empowering**, **encouraging** and **multiplying** believers for ministry in YOUR church!

O O O

1. My church provides written guidelines and procedures for starting new ministries.

Yes ❑   Some Ministries ❑   No ❑   Not Sure ❑

2. Throughout the year, my senior pastor promotes getting involved in ministry through serving.

Regularly ❑   Often ❑   Sometimes ❑   Rarely ❑
Never ❑   Not Sure ❑

3. My church advertises and promotes ways to be involved in serving through ministries.

Regularly ❑   Often ❑   Sometimes ❑   Rarely ❑
Never ❑   Not Sure ❑

4. My church gives proper balance between support and guidance without micro-managing those in ministry positions.

Strongly Agree ❑   Agree ❑   Somewhat Agree/Disagree ❑
Disagree ❑   Strongly Disagree ❑   Not Sure ❑

5. My church staff/leadership gives up responsibilities previously done by them.

Regularly ❑   Often ❑   Sometimes ❑   Rarely ❑
Never ❑   Not Sure ❑

6. My senior pastor and church staff/leadership listen to ministry suggestions and make those who provide them feel valued.

Strongly Agree ❑   Agree ❑   Somewhat Agree/Disagree ❑
Disagree ❑   Strongly Disagree ❑   Not Sure ❑

7. My church provides an intentional process to help members discover their competency and passion to be **empowered** for ministry.

Yes ❑   No ❑   Not Sure ❑

8. My church promotes involvement in ministry BOTH within my church and apart from my church's organized ministries.

Regularly ❑   Often ❑   Sometimes ❑   Rarely ❑
Never ❑   Not Sure ❑

9. My church provides support even when mistakes are made in ministry direction.

Strongly Agree ❑   Agree ❑   Somewhat Agree/Disagree ❑
Disagree ❑   Strongly Disagree ❑   Not Sure ❑

10. My church/ministry leader gives a formal yearly evaluation of each member's ministry.

Regularly ❑   Often ❑   Sometimes ❑   Rarely ❑
Never ❑   Not Sure ❑

11. My church/ministry leader promotes and **encourages** creativity within ministries throughout my church.

Strongly Agree ❑   Agree ❑   Somewhat Agree/Disagree ❑
Disagree ❑   Strongly Disagree ❑   Not Sure ❑

12. My church/ministry leader provides a proper balance between expectations and freedom for carrying out ministry.

Strongly Agree ❑   Agree ❑   Somewhat Agree/Disagree ❑
Disagree ❑   Strongly Disagree ❑   Not Sure ❑

13. My church/ministry leader provides initial and continued training on a regular basis for ministry positions.

Regularly ❑   Often ❑   Sometimes ❑   Rarely ❑
Never ❑   Not Sure ❑

EMPOWERING Evaluation Survey:
For A MINISTRY

O O O

1. My ministry leader provides written guidelines and procedures for starting new ministries.

      Yes ❑   Some Ministries ❑   No ❑   Not Sure ❑

2. Throughout the year, my ministry leader promotes getting involved in ministry through serving.

      Regularly ❑   Often ❑   Sometimes ❑   Rarely ❑
                Never ❑   Not Sure ❑

3. My ministry leader advertises and promotes ways to be involved in serving through ministries.

      Regularly ❑   Often ❑   Sometimes ❑   Rarely ❑
                Never ❑   Not Sure ❑

4. My ministry leader gives proper balance between support and guidance without micro-managing those in ministry positions.

    Strongly Agree ❑   Agree ❑   Somewhat Agree/Disagree ❑
      Disagree ❑   Strongly Disagree ❑   Not Sure ❑

5. My ministry leader gives up responsibilities previously done by him/her.

      Regularly ❑   Often ❑   Sometimes ❑   Rarely ❑
                Never ❑   Not Sure ❑

6. My ministry leader listens to ministry suggestions and makes those who provide them feel valued.

Strongly Agree ❑   Agree ❑   Somewhat Agree/Disagree ❑
Disagree ❑   Strongly Disagree ❑   Not Sure ❑

7. My ministry leader provides an intentional process to help potential volunteers discover their competency and passion to be **empowered** for ministry.

Yes ❑   No ❑   Not Sure ❑

8. My church promotes involvement in ministry BOTH within my church and apart from my church's organized ministries.

Regularly ❑   Often ❑   Sometimes ❑   Rarely ❑
Never ❑   Not Sure ❑

9. My ministry leader provides support even when mistakes are made in ministry direction.

Strongly Agree ❑   Agree ❑   Somewhat Agree/Disagree ❑
Disagree ❑   Strongly Disagree ❑   Not Sure ❑

10. My ministry leader gives a formal yearly evaluation of each member's ministry.

Regularly ❑   Often ❑   Sometimes ❑   Rarely ❑
Never ❑   Not Sure ❑

11. My ministry leader promotes and **encourages** creativity within ministries throughout my church.

Strongly Agree ❑   Agree ❑   Somewhat Agree/Disagree ❑
Disagree ❑   Strongly Disagree ❑   Not Sure ❑

12. My ministry leader provides a proper balance between expectations and freedom for carrying out ministry.

Strongly Agree ❑   Agree ❑   Somewhat Agree/Disagree ❑
Disagree ❑   Strongly Disagree ❑   Not Sure ❑

13. My ministry leader provides initial and continued training on a regular basis for ministry positions.

Regularly ❑   Often ❑   Sometimes ❑   Rarely ❑
Never ❑   Not Sure ❑

Committed to Encouraging God's People for Meaningful Ministry

To **encourage** God's people to serve, start **encouragement** by letting every person know how they fit into the big picture. Most likely, the greatest way those who serve will be **encouraged** to continue is by knowing how they fit into the overall purpose of your church. Those who serve either understand their **connection** to the whole, or they don't.

Life is complicated. There are countless complicated reasons why church members do not serve at all or just give minimal time serving within their churches. However, this book has attempted to uncover and expose the greatest hindrances and obstacles that are created *by those who hold the keys to the gates for unlocking and releasing* God's people into meaningful ministry. Once the *obstacles* are discovered, then *solutions* for church leaders (whether paid or volunteer) can be provided. Ministry leaders will then have to determine whether or not they are committed to removing the obstacles that keep the majority of church members from **connecting** in meaningful ministry.

To review, the first obstacle and corresponding solution centered on being committed to **connecting** God's people to meaningful ministry. The second focused on helping church members intentionally and individually **identify** their unique design by God for ministry. Thirdly, the obstacles and solutions to **equip** God's people were addressed, once they discover where God has led them to make a difference. Next, were the obstacles and solutions to **empower** God's people once they have been **equipped**. Now, the obstacles and solutions need to be directed to those who are already serving. The commitment by ministry leaders must be to **encourage** those already engaged in ministry. If any of these commitments are dealt half-heartedly or with little intentionality, the negative results may not appear immediately, but over time, they will manifest themselves with grave consequences for the Body of Christ.

"And We Appreciate It!"

A few years ago, my wife and I were fulfilling our monthly duty in our church nursery with bed babies. (Yes, to some of you the nursery is not duty, but pure joy.) On this particular Sunday, we had a little boy that cried for over an hour. Finally, the little guy let me hold him and he finally fell asleep while I rocked him. Shortly before my monthly two-hour nursery commitment was up that morning, Mike Schmid, the children's pastor, walked by the door. I jokingly said to Mike, "Just doing ministry, man, just doing ministry!" He was walking past the door, but he came back and replied, "And we appreciate it!" Not a big deal, right? Well maybe not to you, but I have remembered that little **encouragement** for several years now. Four simple words, yet so impactful in **encouraging** me to fulfill a much needed ministry opportunity at my church.

I have told this story to dozens of people at my church. Imagine what happens when Mike does this to the many other workers within the children's ministry. Do you think they tell others about his **encouragement** and possibly even help him recruit? Would his reputation as an **encourager** begin to spread? Would he be able to capitalize on his reputation when recruiting others?

Imagine What Happens through Encouragement or Doesn't Happen without Encouragement

Imagine what happens (maybe it doesn't take much imagination) when those who serve within ministries are never told thank-you and are never **encouraged** for their contributions. Consider the story of the couple who had been married for many years that ended up in a counselor's office with marital problems. The counselor asked the wife to name some of the issues causing the conflict. She said her husband never told her he loved her. The husband looked back at the wife stunned. He told his wife and the counselor that at their wedding, he told her he loved her. He then stated to the counselor, "If I ever changed my mind, I would let her know." Every time I have told or heard the story, the audience laughs. The truth is, this lack of affirmation is not funny. If the truth were known in many churches, those who serve rarely receive **encouragement** and affirmation from ministry leaders once they are recruited for ministry.

A good friend of mine has been highly involved in his church in the past. Several years ago, he told me that when his church first started, he and his wife hosted a dinner for potential new members several times a year. There were 60 to 80 people attending each dinner. At the end, the pastor would share the history of the church's founding, its vision, what was involved in membership and then invite those attending to join the church. My friend told me that never once did the church staff say thank-you or offer to reimburse him for the several hundreds of dollars he and his wife spent for each event. He said, "I would have never taken the money and I do not serve the church for the applause of others, but it would have been nice for the staff to acknowledge the cost associated with the dinners and to say 'thank-you.'"

This morning, Kraig Kelsey, the Executive Director for PLACE Ministries, told me about an event to raise money at his church that took place on Sunday. Kraig was in charge of organizing over 100 people within the church to handle all the logistics for the event. He spent several months in **identifying** and organizing the people for the event. The event was big for the church and big for Kraig, who has been a member of the church for only a year. The church was entrusting Kraig with a big responsibility and he was investing an enormous amount of his time to make sure the logistics of the event ran smoothly. This morning when I asked him how the event went, he told me two or three times about the gratitude he received the previous day from numerous staff members at his church. It was obvious that Kraig was excited that the event was successful, but I could also sense his excitement about the **encouragement** the church staff gave him for his part in the event.

Imagine you attended either the first church where my friend's contributions of time and resources were never acknowledged, or Kraig's church. Assume both churches had dynamic worship services, both were reaching many people for Christ in their communities, the fellowship with fellow believers was incredible (contrary to what some would have us believe, fellowship with other believers is biblical) and the discipleship was strong within both churches. Which church would you rather attend? Have you ever thought that it is fairly easy to pick up on the culture of worship, discipleship, fellowship and evangelism within a church, but it is often hard to pick up on whether the church **encourages** those who are involved? Maybe **encouragement** by ministry leaders to those they oversee is practiced so little that one can only imagine what it looks like fleshed out in the everyday experiences of those who serve within churches.

Membership-Serving Has Its Privileges

Several years ago, American Express ran a commercial with the tag line "Membership has its privileges." As the 60-second commercial was playing, it showed all the benefits of being an American Express cardholder. The aim of the commercial was to get new customers to sign up for American Express credit cards. If churches want to engage more members in ministry, they need to start by **encouraging** the ones already involved in serving.

Studies have shown that a satisfied customer will tell 5–10 other people about their experience. While church members are not customers, the premise is the same—satisfied people tell others about the experience, whether it is buying a car, a house or serving within a church. When recruiting others for ministry, it is far easier when those who are already serving are talking about the **encouragement** they receive from their ministry leaders.

If someone asked those who serve in various capacities at your church, what do you think they would say are the benefits, privileges or positives with regard to serving? After several informal interviews in asking the previous question, rarely has the answer been "the great **encouragement** I have received from my ministry leader."

Why So Little Encouragement?

If my informal survey is correct, we need to ask why ministry leaders offer so little **encouragement** to those who serve within their ministries. If church leaders can realize why they **encourage** so little, then they can make decisions to reverse their actions. For those who are entering ministry where they will have others serving under their leadership, they can begin including **encouragement** from the outset. They can avoid the pitfalls of their predecessors caused by offering little or no **encouragement** to those under their leadership. Many of the reasons why there is so little **encouragement** might start with the phrase:

"Have you ever..."

- ...been around a small child, where no matter what his/her parent did to attempt to get the child to say thank-you to another person, the child refused?

- ...heard these words, "Christians should not work for the applause of others, but for the applause of God?"

- ...heard preachers scold their congregations for not being committed to the church when the preachers arrogantly inform their congregations of their seven-day-a-week commitment?

- ...heard these words, "Whatever you do, work at it with all your heart, as working for the Lord, not for men," (Colossians 3:23) to justify not offering **encouragement** to church members who serve?

- ...heard these words, "Let us not become weary in doing good, for at the proper time we will reap a harvest if we do not give up," (Galatians 6:9) to justify not offering **encouragement** to church members who serve?

Children do not have to be taught to be unappreciative to others. We are born into the world with others taking care of our needs, without having to express gratitude. Without being specifically taught how to express gratitude, many children grow up never learning how to express gratitude to others. Many of these children grow up to become Christians who become leaders who lead church members in ministries within churches.

I have heard Christian leaders quote Colossians 3:23 and Galatians 6:9 as to why they do not applaud their church members for service to the church. In so many cases, people quote Bible verses to fit their preconceived ideas on a particular subject. Many don't quote verses, but have unconsciously developed a mentality that those who serve should not be praised for their service. Their attitude is someone should not be praised for what is expected.

The same ones who use Colossians 3:23 and Galatians 6:9 to justify their lack of **encouragement**, should read passages like Deuteronomy 1:38, 1 Thessalonians 3:2 and Hebrews 3:13. These passages are just a few where leaders like Moses are told by God to **encourage** his assistant Joshua (Deuteronomy 1:38) and leaders like Timothy to **encourage** those at Thessalonica in the faith (1 Thessalonians 3:2). Part of keeping the faith (1 Thessalonians 3:2) is to continue serving where God has called fellow believers to serve. Ministry leaders can do their part of helping fellow believers keep the faith by **encouraging** them. Lastly, the writer of Hebrews 3:13 commanded believers to **encourage** one another daily. This **encouragement** includes ministry leaders **encouraging** those they lead in churches.

How to Encourage Church Members Involved in Ministry

While many ministry leaders may have unconscious reasons as to why they do not **encourage**, most would readily agree they *want* to **encourage**. They want to **encourage** those who so faithfully serve week after week, month after month and year after year in the ministries they oversee. However, they are often unsure of *how* to **encourage** those they lead. It doesn't help when you read books or attend breakout sessions at conferences and are given 1001 ways to **encourage**. Often, we are given so many choices that we do nothing because we feel overwhelmed. The remainder of this chapter is not meant to overwhelm, but to give simple categories to consider when attempting to **encourage** those who serve within your ministry. The chapter will conclude with five simple ways to **encourage** those who serve within churches.

Encouragement Needs to Be Both **Individual** and **Corporate**

Church leaders who oversee church members and staff should **encourage** both individually and corporately, for each yield different benefits for those who serve. When the benefits are combined, a powerful dynamic is unleashed that motivates those who serve to continue with renewed zeal. When either individual or corporate **encouragement** takes place, the overall impact only adds up to equal two when one plus one are added. However, when both are combined, one plus one equals three. Churches that master the art of practicing both have more committed members serving, members that serve longer and the ability to engage more members in meaningful ministry than those who practice one to the exclusion of the other.

Benefits of Individual Encouragement

• God the Father's Example

The example of individual **encouragement** comes from none other than God the Father, Himself. We have to look no further than the example God gave us in Luke 3:22 when He said, "And a voice came from heaven: 'You are my Son, whom I love; with you I am well pleased.'" Have you ever wondered when Christ was being crucified what went through His mind? I would not be surprised if the words spoken by His Father from Luke 3:22 were coming to His thoughts as He was separated from His Father for the first time in eternity.

Ministry leaders need to remember that when they **encourage** church members for a job well done that the benefits last far beyond the words. Just as Jesus likely drew upon His Father's **encouragement** at His greatest time of need, church members need to be able to draw upon words of **encouragement** from their ministry leaders. When church members face difficult challenges in their ministry commitment, it may be words spoken by a ministry leader years earlier that keep them serving.

• Self-Confidence

O O O

Another benefit of **encouraging** church members individually who serve in ministry is the self-confidence that **encouragement** builds for those serving. There are very few people who feel confident in and of themselves when there is a subjective, and at times unmeasurable, analysis of their impact. Those who study the self-esteem of children who grow into adulthood have concluded that children who are affirmed on a regular basis develop far greater self-confidence than those who receive little or sporadic affirmation. If this is true for raising children, the same is true for raising, developing and **encouraging** church members to stay involved and develop skills in ministry areas they serve in.

• Word Spreads from Individuals to Others

O O O

Ministry leaders who **encourage** those who serve in their ministries benefit not only with the individual, but with the network the individual is connected to. There have been numerous studies among sales-driven organizations that prove when a satisfied customer tells so many others about their experience, the testimonial results in more sales. The same is true for ministry servants who are **encouraged** for their contribution. Those **encouraged** will spread the word, which makes it easier to **connect** others in ministry when they are called upon to serve.

Jeff Henderson, the campus pastor for Buckhead Church in Atlanta, related an experience at a conference hosted by Andy Stanley on the impact that **encouraging** others creates beyond the individual. Jeff received information on a first-time guest's experience at Buckhead Church through a posting on a blog site. The guest told of her great experience of interacting with a volunteer on the host team for the church. This first-time guest raved about the helpfulness and politeness of the volunteer.

To **encourage** the volunteer, Jeff printed out the blog comments and added a handwritten note. In the note, he reminded the volunteer what Andy Stanley, the senior pastor, teaches those who volunteer—that the sermon starts in the parking lot. Jeff then wrote, "Apparently, you were preaching a whale of a sermon because you are now famous on a blog site. Thank-you, thank-you, thank-you for what you are doing. I count it a privilege to serve alongside you at Buckhead Church." (Henderson and Stanley, 2006) Andy returned this comment: "I guarantee you, Burien [the volunteer] communicates that Jeff, our senior leader at Buckhead Church, is paying attention." (ibid.)

Benefits of Corporate Encouragement

• Connected to a Mission Bigger Than Oneself

When a person serving in ministry is **encouraged** with a group, the impact is felt in the entire group's accomplishment, not just the one person's contribution. A couple of years ago, the ministers at my church met with those who sit down one-on-one with church members looking for a place to serve and informed us of the impact we made in the lives of multiple ministries within our church. They told us the overall impact of our contribution and they told us specific instances where what we did made a difference in their ministries and the lives impacted outside the church walls. We heard about the impact as a group. We walked out of the meeting knowing that as a group we were making a significant impact at our church and on the Kingdom.

• Opportunities to Support Others' Responsibilities

When people are **encouraged** corporately, there is the opportunity not only to know what others are doing, but to realize ways to help one another. Capital stewardship campaigns have utilized the giving of some to spur others to share in the privilege and responsibility of giving. In many capital campaigns, there is an advance dinner where those who attend make commitments. These commitments are collectively made known to the entire church with the hopes of **encouraging** others to join in the campaign to raise financial resources for the church. The same effect takes place when ministry leaders collectively **encourage** those who serve. Not only are those already serving **encouraged**, but they are often able to realize ways to support others in their ministries.

• Corporate Encouragement Propels an Attitude of Success

When those who serve within churches are **encouraged** corporately and publicly as a group, it creates an environment of success. The old saying, "perception creates reality," can be helpful or harmful. In the context of building a culture for **connecting** God's people into meaningful ministry, **encouraging** them publicly as a group is a great way to build a church. If the **encouragement** is warranted and not just flattery, then it will be a powerful motivator for those who serve and for those not yet serving.

I have a pastor friend who, on a regular basis, uses the platform on Sunday morning to criticize his congregation for not doing enough. My pastor friend has been fixated for years on having a church much larger than the one he is currently serving and has for many years. While he has never asked me for my opinion on why his church has never grown to what he envisioned when he became pastor, I certainly have a definite opinion. If he asked, I would suggest he choose a church member that would have the controls for an electrical shock zapper that was attached to my pastor friend. Every time the pastor expressed criticism, the member with the zapper would send a jolt through the pastor! My guess is that within a short time, the pastor would be cured of his uncontrolled urge to criticize those within the church! Also, I would predict that the church would then reach the goals and aspirations he envisioned years ago.

Obviously, my zapper idea for negative pastors is a little unrealistic. However, what could be realistic would be to have someone within the congregation for a certain period of time assigned to chart pertinent categories like criticism vs. **encouragement** of the congregation by the senior pastor. There are MANY reasons churches stagnate, plateau or decline, but my guess is that one of the major causes of stagnated and declining churches is a lack of corporate and public **encouragement**.

Finally, if the senior pastor's staff or inner circle are not being **encouraged** privately, publicly and corporately, then the ripple effect will spread even if the entire church is unaware of the lack of **encouragement** by the senior pastor. A staff member does not even have to verbally acknowledge the pastor's lack of **encouragement** for the church to become an environment where **encouragement** is not part of the culture. When those who are natural **encouragers** serve with a senior pastor who is not often the **encourager**, they become like the senior pastor and refrain from **encouraging**.

I once asked a staff member why he followed the lead of his senior pastor in not **encouraging**. He said that he and others on the staff didn't want to make the senior pastor look bad by showing such a disparity between their actions and the senior pastor's actions. How sad! The real tragedy lies with those who were faithfully serving within his church without being **encouraged**.

Encouragement Should Be Specific

Encouragement to those who serve needs to be specific and not always general. General **encouragement** would be something like, "You are a great asset to this ministry." There's nothing wrong with this type of **encouragement**, but there also needs to be specific instances and reasons for the **encouragement**.

Several weeks ago, I spoke to my Bible study class regarding the need to view our jobs as more than a place to get a paycheck to pay bills. My challenge to the class was to view our jobs as the place God wants to use us to make a difference in His Kingdom. Two weeks later, a doctor in my class thanked me for helping him to realize there was a calling beyond his making sure people fall asleep before surgery. He went on to talk about what God was teaching him about his calling as a doctor. I would have been grateful if he had told me, "Great teaching a couple of weeks ago on calling," but I was super **encouraged** when he *specifically* told me how my speaking impacted him.

- **Encouragement** that is always GENERAL by ministry leaders becomes hollow.
- **Encouragement** that is always GENERAL comes across as insincere.
- **Encouragement** that is always GENERAL will often be discarded as fake.

- **Encouragement** that is SPECIFIC will come across as genuine.
- **Encouragement** that is SPECIFIC will comes across as heart-felt.
- **Encouragement** that is SPECIFIC will comes across as sincere.
- **Encouragement** that is SPECIFIC will come across as thoughtful.

Encouragement Needs to Be Planned and Intentional

If you have been attending church for more than a year, you have most likely heard these words by a senior pastor, "If you want to know what is important to you, then look at your calendar and your checkbook." Truer words could not have been spoken when determining whether a church has a culture that **encourages** those who serve within the ministries at the church.

Biltmore Baptist Church in Asheville, North Carolina **encourages** their volunteers annually with an awards ceremony called "The Light Awards." I attended their Second Annual Light Awards. It was unbelievable how awe-inspiring the event was to me and my staff who also attended. As the volunteers arrived, they were greeted by staff members wearing long evening dresses and tuxedos along a walkway lined with red carpet. The staff, their spouses and children served an incredible meal to over 700 volunteers that night.

After the meal, there was entertainment and an awards ceremony for the five ministry objectives of the church. There was video, along with drama, to highlight the impact within the church, community and beyond for each of the five ministry objectives. At the end of highlighting each ministry objective, the staff member over that ministry area would give an award to a volunteer who went above and beyond in that ministry area. The volunteer accepted the award on behalf of that ministry area.

The end of the evening culminated with James Walker, the senior pastor at Biltmore, giving a 10 minute message **encouraging** and validating those who volunteer at Biltmore. Right before the close of the evening, he asked the staff, support staff, their spouses and children (over 150 individuals) to come on the stage. James closed by pointing at the volunteers sitting and said, "This one's for you." He begin to clap along with the other 150 onstage. They clapped for over two minutes. To this day, I have chills remembering that night. Biltmore has found an intentional way to **encourage** those who serve.

> *Does your church or ministry's budget and calendar have built into them ways to appreciate and **encourage** those who serve?*

Does your church or ministry's budget and calendar have built into them ways to appreciate and **encourage** those who serve?

Encouragement Needs to Be **Regular** and **Unpredictable**

For many years, my aunt has called me on my birthday and sung me a happy birthday jingle she made up. A few years ago, she did not call, and to say I was disappointed was an understatement. I have looked forward to hearing that little birthday song as much as any present I receive. Thankfully, her birthday song (**encouragement**) that I missed for one year has returned with the last few birthdays. Ministry leaders who desire to keep those serving with them will look for special occasions like birthdays, anniversary serving dates, etc. to **encourage** those who serve alongside them. There is a section in www.mobilyzr.com that gives ministry leaders the capability to be automatically notified of serving anniversary dates of those who serve within their ministries. Whenever **encouragement** is provided on a regular basis, whether it be a church or ministry-wide event, it is important to remember that people create expectations based on performance. In others words, to start a regular event and then to stop it will often do more harm than if the **encouragement** had never been started. The phrase "under-commit and over-deliver" needs to be remembered when providing regular **encouragement** to those who serve in ministry.

While people do enjoy regular, predictable **encouragement**, it will also be important, at times, for no specific reason, to provide **encouragement** to those who serve. As I was writing the previous sentence, my cell phone rang. The call was from a pastor that in the past made regular monthly and sometimes weekly calls to me. Several months ago, my advice, opinion, or whatever one might label it, was not received warmly by this pastor. I had not called him, nor had he called me since then, but I have continued to receive his newsletter. The previous week, I read where he graduated with his masters in biblical studies. I immediately wrote him a note congratulating him on his graduation. The day he received the note, he picked up the phone and called me to say thanks for the **encouraging** note. While I did not ask my pastor friend, I could tell by his response that he was surprised with my unpredictable letter of **encouragement**.

Combine regular, predictable **encouragement** with irregular, unpredictable times of **encouragement** and watch those who serve blossom with excitement, commitment and impact in the areas they serve.

Mix Encouragement with **Correction** and **Improvement**

If you have ever taken a visit to the business section of a bookstore and looked at books on how to conduct job performance appraisals for employees, several guidelines are consistent in all the books. One example is to mix in the evaluation what the employee does that is positive with areas the employee needs improvement. While one seems to be positive and the correction may appear to be negative, the reality is both are positive. Most who serve in ministry desire to excel and improve their impact through their service. When only the areas they excel in are highlighted with praise and **encouragement**, their ceiling for greater impact is not to the level it could be with positive, constructive areas for improvement.

Five Ways to Appreciate Those Who Serve

For several years, my wife and I worked with young single adults and engaged couples at several churches in Georgia, California and Oklahoma. We also had the opportunity to lead retreats for couples throughout the United States and even overseas. One afternoon, I was looking at all the resources and books I had studied for teaching on relationships. I counted the books in my library and realized I had read over 300 books on relationships. Of all those books, there is one book that has been more valuable than all the others combined. The book is *The Five Love Languages* written by Dr. Gary Chapman. The premise of the book is people give and receive love in one of five ways. The five love languages are:

1. Words of Affirmation
2. Acts of Service
3. Receiving Gifts
4. Quality Time
5. Touch

For the purposes of our subject matter—**encouraging** God's people in meaningful ministry—we will refer to Chapman's five love languages as five ways to encourage those who serve in ministry. After all, ministry is about relationships. The tag on the front of the book after the title is *"How to Express Heartfelt Commitment to Your Mate."* Whether you refer to the five elements as ways to express **encouragement** or heartfelt commitment to those who serve under you, it will have a powerful impact if you discover and practice these five elements in your ministry. Applying them beyond those within your ministry, it will also impact every relationship you have, if you discover and practice these five ways to express commitment to others.

It doesn't take a sociologist to determine that the most difficult, yet rewarding, relationship is between a couple, especially those who enter into a marriage relationship. If these five ways to express commitment to a spouse can fill his/her emotional love tank, think how powerful the impact can be when incorporating these elements into how a ministry leader expresses **encouragement** and gratitude to those who serve within his/her ministry. The dividends will be incalculable.

1. **Encouragement** through **Words of Affirmation** – words that **encourage** or compliment a ministry worker.

O O O

"Mark Twain once said, 'I can live for two months on a good compliment.' If we take Twain literally, six compliments a year would have kept his emotional love tank at the operational level." (Chapman, 1992, p. 39). There are countless men and women, boys and girls that serve week after week in ministry that would say amen to Mark Twain's statement. The book of Proverbs has several themes woven throughout the 31 chapters. One theme is the power that words have to build up and tear down (Proverbs 10:21, Proverbs 10:31, Proverbs 12:18, Proverbs 15:23 and Proverbs 18:21). Proverbs 16:24 says, "Pleasant words are a honeycomb, sweet to the soul and healing to the bones."

2. **Encouragement** through **Acts of Service** – physically doing something for a ministry worker.

O O O

This type of **encouragement** has been referred to earlier when presenting servant leadership as a way to **equip** those within your ministry. A simple example would be a ministry leader who walks into a class room on Sunday morning and helps the Sunday School teacher clean up.

One of the primary ways my wife feels cared for is when I help her through acts of service. Her least favorite way to feel appreciated is through words of affirmation, which is my primary way to feel appreciated. I help oversee ministry placement at my church and my wife serves on the team I help lead. For me to tell her she did a great job in her ministry task does not encourage her nearly as much as when I physically do something to help with her tasks.

3. **Encouragement** through **Quality Time** – giving a ministry worker undivided attention.

A ministry leader can **encourage** endlessly through words of affirmation, helping a Sunday School teacher clean classrooms or whatever the leader might do through acts of service and still do very little to **encourage** those who serve if their primary way to be **encouraged** is through quality time. In a recent conversation with a young man who is part of a new church, he complained about his pastor with regard to time. The young man said, "I want to sit down with the pastor and talk to him about what is going on with me and the ministry I am helping oversee at the church." The young man is considered part of the pastor's inner core of leaders. The pastor would be wise to spend quality time with the young man in meaningful conversation. Given quality time with the pastor, the young man who is a leader in the church would leave **encouraged** and energized to lead with a renewed passion for the church and his ministry.

4. **Encouragement** through **Gifts** –
providing something that a ministry worker can hold in his/her hand that is given by the ministry leader.

O O O

Dr. Chapman says,

> "A gift is something you can hold in your hand and say, 'Look, he was thinking of me,' or, 'She remembered me.' You must be thinking of someone to give him a gift. The gift itself is a symbol of that thought. It doesn't matter whether it cost money. What is important is that you thought of him. And it is not the thought implanted only in the mind that counts, but the thought expressed in actually securing the gift and giving it as the expression of love." (ibid., 74–75)

Let me personally illustrate the power gifts have to impact relationships, whether discussing family relationships or relationships from ministry leaders to ministry workers. My primary love language is words of affirmation and my dad's primary love language is gifts. For many years, I was frustrated and angry at times that my dad did not regularly affirm me as a son and partner with him in business. When I came to understand that my dad showed his love to me through gifts (he has provided incredible opportunities for me through his financial support to my ministry), it changed my entire relationship with my dad. Not only do I understand how my dad expresses his commitment to me, but I now know how to express love, **encouragement** and gratitude to my dad.

My dad loves horses. He sponsors a horse camp that my children and their friends participate in at no cost to my kids or their friends. To tell my dad how awesome he is for sponsoring this camp would have very little meaning to him. However, for the kids to make him a present around the theme of horses and then present it to my dad—speaks volumes.

Transition from relationships with parents and horse camps to those who serve in ministries throughout churches. When a ministry leader knows that those within his/her ministry receive **encouragement** through gifts, then it becomes a given that those who serve under the ministry leader will feel **encouraged** through gifts. Gifts will be a part of keeping and sustaining the ministry worker. Gifts will be a part of motivating the ministry worker to excel. Gifts will be a part of energizing the ministry worker.

5. **Encouragement** through **Physical Touch** –
a simple, yet powerful gesture to **encourage** those who serve.

Have you ever heard these words when people have a positive encounter with each other, "I hope you don't mind, but I am a hugger"? From there, the person reaches out and hugs the person the comment is directed to. Most likely, when you hear those words, there is a very good chance the person making them would receive **encouragement** through simple gestures like placing his/her hand on someone to compliment them. Obviously, when dealing with someone of the opposite sex, there needs to be discretion where physical touch is associated. However, in appropriate settings and in appropriate ways, touch is a powerful way for ministry leaders to **encourage** those who serve under them.

How to Discover the Five Ways to Encourage

Some people are more perceptive and intuitive than others. Some people can remember what others tell them about themselves. However, for the majority of ministry leaders, perception and a photographic memory of how those who serve under them feel **encouraged** is not going to happen automatically. There needs to be an intentional way for leaders to discover and remember each individual's primary way to be **encouraged**.

I have heard hundreds of times from people that they can't remember their primary personality type or spiritual gifts—just days after taking inventories to discover them. If people can't remember something about themselves, how successful will they be in remembering specific information about those who serve within their ministries?

Earlier in the **equipping** chapter, we suggested surveying the ways people like to be **equipped**. We recommend doing the same with those who serve under ministry leaders by having them rank from 1 to 5 how they are most **encouraged** according to Dr. Chapman's five ways. I have asked literally hundreds of individuals what they believe their primary love language is by giving a one sentence or less description of the five. Over 90 percent of the time, people have been able to immediately identify their primary ways to be appreciated. It is highly recommended that if you are a ministry leader looking for ways to encourage those you lead, then read *The Five Love Languages*. While reading it, substitute ministry workers for spouses and reflect on examples that have to do with **encouraging** those who serve within your ministry.

Conclusion

The beginning of this chapter brought up all the books and conferences that give 1001 practical ways to energize, **encourage**, appreciate, motivate or influence those you are leading. These countless ways will take on new significance when they can be categorized and matched to those who feel appreciated, primarily through one of five ways. Expressing thank-you in these specific ways will take on increased impact.

This chapter focused on why **encouragement** by those who lead others in ministry is often withheld. It attempted to show the benefit for both the ministry leader and the ministry worker who gives and receives **encouragement**. It concluded with providing practical ways for ministry leaders to give **encouragement** to ministry workers. It would be naïve to believe all that needs to be written on **encouraging** those who serve in ministry has been written in these few pages. It is hoped that these insights will be useful and become a starting point, but most importantly, allow God through His Holy Spirit to guide your thoughts and actions in seeking ways to **encourage** those who serve in ministry.

ENCOURAGING Evaluation Survey:
For A CHURCH

O O O

To take the evaluations and score yourself, look on the reverse side of the back jacket of this book. You will find a user ID and password. Go to this website: *http://www.mobilyzr.com/ evaluations* and insert your user ID and password. Additional instructions are on the website. Once you are taking the evaluations on the website, the results will be graphed. In this book, you can review the evaluations, but not score yourself or those who take them as a group. Also, there is the opportunity to purchase evaluations and divide them into groups to also assess the effectiveness of various groups within your church or ministry regarding **encouraging** God's people for meaningful ministry.

The evaluations are brief and simple, yet the results can be life-changing for you and your church. Invest just a few minutes of time so you can **identify** where you are and what your next steps need to be in **connecting**, **identifying**, **equipping**, **empowering**, **encouraging** and **multiplying** believers for ministry in YOUR church!

O O O

1. My church provides a culture of **encouragement** to those serving in ministry.

Strongly Agree ❑   Agree ❑   Somewhat Agree/Disagree ❑
Disagree ❑   Strongly Disagree ❑   Not Sure ❑

2. My church has a yearly event outside of normal church activities to recognize those serving in ministry.

Yes ❑   No ❑   Not Sure ❑

3. At least once a year, my church has a time during normal church activities to recognize those serving in ministry.

Yes ❑   No ❑   Not Sure ❑

4. My church has a strategy for **encouraging** members involved in ministry.

Strongly Agree ❑   Agree ❑   Somewhat Agree/Disagree ❑
Disagree ❑   Strongly Disagree ❑   Not Sure ❑

5. My church highlights those serving in ministry through various communication tools.

Regularly ❑   Often ❑   Sometimes ❑   Rarely ❑
Never ❑   Not Sure ❑

6. My church provides training for those involved in ministry.

Strongly Agree ❑   Agree ❑   Somewhat Agree/Disagree ❑
Disagree ❑   Strongly Disagree ❑   Not Sure ❑

7. My church **encourages** potential volunteers to discover their competency and passion for ministry before engaging in a ministry position.

Strongly Agree ❑   Agree ❑   Somewhat Agree/Disagree ❑
Disagree ❑   Strongly Disagree ❑   Not Sure ❑

8. My church **encourages** ministry participation based on passion and not on guilt.

Strongly Agree ❑   Agree ❑   Somewhat Agree/Disagree ❑
Disagree ❑   Strongly Disagree ❑   Not Sure ❑

9. My church **encourages** members to serve both within and outside the church.

Strongly Agree ❑   Agree ❑   Somewhat Agree/Disagree ❑
Disagree ❑   Strongly Disagree ❑   Not Sure ❑

10. My church budget underwrites training for ministry workers.

Always ❑   Almost Always ❑   Often ❑   Sometimes ❑
Rarely ❑   Never ❑   Not Sure ❑

11. My church **encourages** ministry workers to get together for fellowship and not just ministry tasks or training.

Strongly Agree ❑   Agree ❑   Somewhat Agree/Disagree ❑
Disagree ❑   Strongly Disagree ❑   Not Sure ❑

12. My church shows appreciation for those stepping down from ministry positions.

Strongly Agree ❑   Agree ❑   Somewhat Agree/Disagree ❑
Disagree ❑   Strongly Disagree ❑   Not Sure ❑

13. My church annually evaluates if our ministry workers are over-committed in their ministries.

Strongly Agree ❑   Agree ❑   Somewhat Agree/Disagree ❑
Disagree ❑   Strongly Disagree ❑   Not Sure ❑

14. My church **encourages** ministry workers to grow in their personal relationship with God.

Strongly Agree ❑   Agree ❑   Somewhat Agree/Disagree ❑
Disagree ❑   Strongly Disagree ❑   Not Sure ❑

ENCOURAGING Evaluation Survey:
For A MINISTRY

O O O

1. My ministry provides a culture of **encouragement** to those serving in ministry.

   Strongly Agree ❏   Agree ❏   Somewhat Agree/Disagree ❏
   Disagree ❏   Strongly Disagree ❏   Not Sure ❏

2. My ministry has a yearly event outside of normal church activities to recognize those serving in ministry.

   Yes ❏   No ❏   Not Sure ❏

3. At least once a year, my ministry has a time during normal church activities to recognize those serving in ministry.

   Yes ❏   No ❏   Not Sure ❏

4. My ministry has a strategy for **encouraging** members involved in ministry.

   Strongly Agree ❏   Agree ❏   Somewhat Agree/Disagree ❏
   Disagree ❏   Strongly Disagree ❏   Not Sure ❏

5. My ministry highlights those serving in ministry through various communication tools.

   Regularly ❏   Often ❏   Sometimes ❏   Rarely ❏
   Never ❏   Not Sure ❏

6. My ministry provides training for those involved in ministry.

Strongly Agree ❑   Agree ❑   Somewhat Agree/Disagree ❑
Disagree ❑   Strongly Disagree ❑   Not Sure ❑

7. My ministry **encourages** potential volunteers to discover their competency and passion for ministry before engaging in a ministry position.

Strongly Agree ❑   Agree ❑   Somewhat Agree/Disagree ❑
Disagree ❑   Strongly Disagree ❑   Not Sure ❑

8. My ministry **encourages** ministry participation based on passion and not on guilt.

Strongly Agree ❑   Agree ❑   Somewhat Agree/Disagree ❑
Disagree ❑   Strongly Disagree ❑   Not Sure ❑

9. My ministry **encourages** members to serve both within and outside the church.

Strongly Agree ❑   Agree ❑   Somewhat Agree/Disagree ❑
Disagree ❑   Strongly Disagree ❑   Not Sure ❑

10. My ministry budget underwrites training for ministry workers.

Always ❑   Almost Always ❑   Often ❑   Sometimes ❑
Rarely ❑   Never ❑   Not Sure ❑

11. My ministry **encourages** ministry workers to get together for fellowship and not just ministry tasks or training.

Strongly Agree ❑   Agree ❑   Somewhat Agree/Disagree ❑
Disagree ❑   Strongly Disagree ❑   Not Sure ❑

Committed to Multiplying God's People for Meaningful Ministry

2 Timothy 2:2 – "And the things you have heard me say in the presence of many witnesses entrust to reliable men who will also be qualified to teach others."

What do Kurt Warner (1999 and 2001 NFL MVP), Herschel Walker (1982 Heisman Trophy Winner) and Dwayne Wade (2006 NBA Final MVP) have in common? Most would correctly assume that they have dominated their sports at some point in their careers. However, all three were at one time not listed as number one on the depth chart of their respective teams.

In 1980, I was a teammate with Herschel Walker at the University of Georgia. Our season opener that year was with the University of Tennessee in Knoxville. In the third quarter, we were down 15–0. The coaches made a decision to put in Herschel. Even though he had been the most highly recruited player out of high school the year before, he had not met expectations in practice and was listed as the number three running back on the depth chart. Herschel came into the game, scored two touchdowns and we won 16–15. The rest is history, as Georgia went on to an undefeated season that year and won the national championship. Herschel went on to become, according to ESPN, the greatest college running back ever to play college football.

I have watched several television specials over the years about Herschel. I have never seen one that tells about his career starting at the University of Georgia as the third string running back going into the first game. As it relates to this book, why is it important to recount this story? Herschel, along with Dwayne Wade and Kurt Warner and multitudes of athletes, started their careers behind someone else only to propel to stardom when given the opportunity. The point is, they were coached for the moment they would have the opportunity to excel. The mantle was passed from their predecessor to them and from them to those who followed them.

From Sports to Church

Whether it is professional sports, business or the government, all entities must plan for an event—like the succession of power. If something should happen to the president, there must always be a plan for those who would succeed the ones on the front line. Unfortunately, this is not the way most churches operate when it comes to those who fulfill ministry responsibilities.

It has been said that whether someone acknowledges the source of truth, all truth flows from God's directives to His people in the Bible. This could not be truer than when observing the succession of many businesses, sports teams and governments around the world. These groups practice the truth taught in 2 Timothy 2:2 (what I have taught you, teach others who can teach others), both in word and action, when it comes to planning for succession. Sadly, many churches have acknowledged the truth Paul gave to Timothy in 2 Timothy 2:2, but only sporadically practice it. Rarely is it practiced with intentionality. Some churches have certain ministries that practice 2 Timothy 2:2 and completely ignore it for others.

Churches that take the commitment seriously to **connect** God's people to meaningful ministry, will need to incorporate an intentional strategy to **multiply** and add more ministry workers. **Multiplication's** importance for the continuing future of the Church has been taught for years as it relates to reaching non-Christians or transferring biblical truth from one generation to another. Rarely is **multiplication** taught as it relates to **connecting** believers into meaningful ministry and its relevance to the future of Christianity.

Take a Test

Take an informal test of your church or ministry. How many ministries and/or individuals do you know that are officially being mentored to **multiply** the ministry or person training them? When answering the question, keep in mind it is not to just be mentored to perform a job, task or responsibility, but to learn it and transfer it to another person. For example, I committed to disciple four men at a new church. In recruiting these men and others who are to be part of the discipleship process, the pastor agreed that after one year, they in turn would disciple others. If only two of my four men follow through in a year, my efforts will equate to eight new men being mentored. If several of these mentor others, then my mentoring four men will continue to **multiply**.

Another example is those at my church who desire to be one-on-one coaches in helping members **connect** to meaningful ministry. These potential coaches have to meet the following qualifications:

1. Attend a PLACE workshop at our church as a participant.

2. Have a coach within our church work through the potential coach's profile as if the potential coach were a participant looking to serve within our church.

3. Read several books that are provided by the church on coaching and interpreting the PLACE profile.

4. Watch a video on the one-on-one training for coaches.

5. As a silent observer, watch two one-on-one coaching sessions by a trained consultant and process the session at the end, both with the participant and the trainer.

6. Conduct two coaching sessions with a trained coach as a silent observer and process the session at the end, both with the participant and the trainer.

7. Conduct 4–6 coaching sessions to determine whether the ministry opportunity is one they desire to continue.

The above **equipping** process can take from three to six months to complete. While this seems like an enormous investment of time, the ministry to **connect** church members to meaningful ministry has a good indication of the person's ability to perform the ministry task. The potential coach has a good idea of what is involved and whether he/she is suited for the ministry. If both the ministry coach and the person agree there is a fit, then the **equipping** process has **multiplied** another person for meaningful ministry. The person the coach **identifies** for ministry will most likely impact many others that he/she engages at the church or in ministry outside the walls of the church.

Imagine the scope and breadth of impact that churches could and would make if once a year, they examined their existing ministries and determined how many people were training and **multiplying** others.

Character Development, Biblical Worldview and Ministry Involvement

My spiritual father, Grady Roan, died in 1994. He was pastor of First Baptist Church in Vidalia, Georgia for 18 years. One of my greatest honors in life was when his wife asked me to conduct his funeral with the associate pastor. The pallbearers were men who had gone into full-time vocational ministry that had come out of the church under Grady Roan's leadership. There were close to 100 men. I knew many others who could not attend, but had also been inspired while he was the pastor and were now serving in many places around the world.

After the funeral, I compared Grady Roan's pastorate with that of another pastor—same denomination, but one of the largest churches in their denomination. The other pastor's church was 7–8 times larger than Grady's in attendance and baptized more than tenfold the number baptized at Grady's church. While the other pastor had a larger church with more baptisms, I discovered that each year, Grady's church sent 3–4 times more men and women to seminary and into full-time missions than the larger church.

Most would believe the larger church was impacting eternity to a greater degree. I look forward to getting to heaven and asking God whose ministry impacted more people for eternity. I will not be surprised if Grady Roan's ministry has influenced more people for eternity. He continues to impact life on earth through men and women like myself, even years after his death.

Grady Roan's specialty was mentoring men like myself in an informal manner, mainly in character development and in develop-ing a biblical worldview. At the same time, Don Moye, the minister of music and youth, was mentoring me and many others in a struc-tured manner in character development, a biblical worldview and ministry involvement. For two years, I served under Don where I learned how to grow in my own individual walk with God and in how to lead others to grow in their spiritual lives. Don would meet with the interns and others throughout the church, both as a group and individually. In turn, those who met with Don would duplicate what he was doing with us, and the power and reach of the minis-try was **multiplied**.

Sadly, much of the mentoring that takes place today is either/ or and not both/and, like the mentoring I received at First Baptist Church in Vidalia, Georgia. What is meant by either/or? Much of the mentoring today separates character development, teaching on a biblical worldview and ministry involvement.

For example, I listened to a conference where a well-known church was teaching other churches about their volunteer process. Not one time in the discussion was it ever mentioned that those who train others in ministry involvement should also help those serving develop in character and a biblical worldview. This well-known church does a good job in **multiplying** their members to perform ministry tasks, but apparently does very little in developing their character and biblical worldview through their training to serve on ministry teams. Even if my assumption regarding this church is wrong, they did not consider it important enough to discuss when teaching other churches how to create a volunteer process that involves more than the transfer of ministry skills. In days gone by, they were seen as one in the same and not separate processes.

Recently, I was speaking in my home church and talked with Jeff McLain, now a respected businessman and deacon within the church. We talked about his and his brother's spiritual journeys, both of which I had the privilege of investing in while they were in high school and I was a youth intern under Don Moye. His brother, Dr. Marty McLain, is now the senior pastor of First Baptist Church in Lithia Springs, Georgia. The **multiplication** process of Grady Roan and Don Moye has extended beyond their personal impact to men like myself who then transferred what I was taught to men like Jeff and Marty McLain.

Multiplication through Students

Just a few years ago, many of the leading churches that influenced other churches, incorporated the **multiplication** process that is providing dividends to churches today. The process would find students that had a hot heart for God and ministry and seek to disciple them apart from the other students. These students, in turn, would disciple their peers (2 Timothy 2:2).

My first position as a student minister came in 1984. After my first year in seminary, I was called to be the student minister at the First Baptist Church in Mineral Wells, Texas. The church had approximately 115 students on roll—most were actual members and some were regular attendees, but not members. Six months into my position, I recruited four young adults, who along with myself, took all 115 students and assessed where they were in their spiritual development. (This was years before I heard about Rick Warren's core, committed, congregation, crowd, community [1995].) We determined which students we felt would respond positively to which adult. Our goal with the students who had very little interest in spiritual matters was to move them closer to a desire for God. We wanted to have those who were not far away from mentoring others to develop a desire, along with training, to disciple their peers. Our eventual goal was to see those who we started with, who had little interest in spiritual matters, growing to a desire to mentor others.

We divided the students into four groups according to their spiritual hunger for God. Each adult leader had between 20-25 students and we met individually with 4–6 students each week to disciple them. These 4-6 students demonstrated a hot heart for God and a desire to grow in godly character and ministry involvement (yes, even teenagers have a desire to serve God by being the hands and feet of Jesus). They, in turn, begin to disciple others that had a desire to grow spiritually through discipleship (2 Timothy 2:2).

It should be noted that the adult leaders I recruited met every other Thursday night with me. Not only did we discuss where our students were in their spiritual journeys, but the four adults and I also worked through discipleship material to help us grow in our own spiritual journeys. In other words, what we were teaching the students, we were practicing in our own lives (2 Timothy 2:2).

Several of the students from that church have gone on to become vocational ministers. Ten years after leaving First Baptist Church in Mineral Wells, Texas, I was attending a Steve Farrar Men's Conference at my church in Atlanta. A young man in his mid-20s walked up to me and introduced himself. He said he was best friends with Shannon Hart while growing up in Mineral Wells. He went on to tell me that he attended many events at First Baptist while I was the student pastor, but what he admired more than the events was the discipleship that Shannon and other students at First Baptist received.

He told me his last week with Steve Farrar Ministries was this conference I was attending. The following week, he was getting married and moving to Dallas, Texas to become a youth minister. I will never forget his next words. He said, "Thank-you for the example I saw in your youth ministry. I am going to design mine exactly like I saw you do at First Baptist." My first thought was, "Thank-you Don Moye for teaching me and practicing 2 Timothy 2:2 while I was serving under you as an intern while in college."

First Impressions Last a Lifetime

Studies have shown that the first five years of life shape a person throughout their lifetime. The environment they are exposed to has enormous influence on how they think, what they value and ultimately who they become. There are exceptions, but studies show those who break from the environment they were exposed to as children are often rare. These first impressions go far beyond the first five years of life. They go on to what and how a person is trained in their first job, either from a positive shaping or to a negative shaping. First impressions are seen in college students in how they view the world as they leave their parents' influence. First impressions are also shaped when a person gets serious about their relationship with Christ or commits their life to Christ.

In my own experience, I thought all new Christians were taught 2 Timothy 2:2 because that is what I was exposed to through my home church, Fellowship of Christian Athletes and Campus Crusade for Christ. When I became a Christian in college, my home church and these two organizations strongly taught and practiced 2 Timothy 2:2. I assumed this was how all churches taught and passed along truth. I was deeply disappointed when I left the nest and flew away from the influence of these groups. I realized it was not a given that every church practiced 2 Timothy 2:2.

Unfortunately, many of the leading churches no longer practice 2 Timothy 2:2 with those within their student ministries. I have worked with thousands of churches since the late 1990s. Rarely have I seen 2 Timothy 2:2 practiced in student ministry, with it being even rarer with adults.

Recently, I was talking with one of the pastors at my church about this sad observation. His daughter is going into the eleventh grade and would be considered a godly young lady with a hot heart for God and spiritual matters. I asked him if there is ever a time where his daughter, and truly spiritual students like her, are ever separated from the kids who attend because parents make them attend and they obviously have no desire for spiritual matters. He said no. I have asked that question dozens and dozens of times to church leaders across the country and 99% of the time the answer has been no.

Who Shall Lead Them?

In 2005, Larry A. Witham and Oxford University Press released a fascinating book entitled *Who Shall Lead Them? The Future of Ministry in America*. The book focused on the history of clergy in the United States, along with the present state of clergy and what might be the future of clergy in the United States.

Witham predicted,

> "With the present low recruitment levels, the day
> might come when most American churches have
> no ordained ministers in their pulpits. At present,
> the number of clergy under age thirty is remarkably
> small. Ordinations today average in the mid-thir-
> ties. 'The death of young clergy sounds a wake-up
> call to the already called,' said one young minister.
> 'Pastors have a crucial role to play in stimulating
> the vocational imagination of the youth in their
> congregations.' He cited an estimate that if just 10
> percent of pastors raised up a young apprentice, 'the
> tide would turn.'" (Witham, 2005, p. 192)

While *Are You Committed?* is not about the future of clergy in America, we know that what starts (or does not start) in the pulpit trickles down to the pew. If young people do not enter vocational ministry, spreading Christianity in North America will become increasingly harder as we pass the faith from generation to genera- tion. *Are You Committed?* is about **connecting** God's people into meaningful ministry. Without strong leadership from pastors, the ability to influence God's people to **connect** and then **multiply** themselves will be greatly diminished.

On the positive side, with strong leaders who will take God at His word and incorporate 2 Timothy 2:2, the tide can be reversed. As with any challenge, the first step to correcting it is to recognize what the challenge is and then have a willingness to make corrections. When it comes to **multiplying** God's people for meaningful ministry, the first step is to recognize the lack of emphasis on this biblical principle. Next, church leaders need to simply incorporate 2 Timothy 2:2 in the ministry involvement strategy of their churches.

Incorporating the New with the Old

Recently, my dad and I were driving to a baseball game to watch the Atlanta Braves. While driving, we passed several government buildings, some of which were named after men my dad has personally known. He related several stories about these men and their impact on both him and the state of Georgia. As we were entering the stadium, he made a comment that will always stick with me. He said, "Life used to be much simpler. If we could incorporate the relational simplicity of the past with all the modern technology of today, our society could be something special."

> *Tracking improvement is a major key as to how effective the **multiplication** of God's people for meaningful ministry is at your church.*

His statement had huge implications in my mind as it relates to **multiplying** God's people for meaningful ministry. In days gone by, mentoring others for ministry was relatively simple because it was easier to observe and interact with those whom we mentored. Not only was life not as busy, but there were fewer people to manage. Today, with the rise of busy lifestyles, along with many larger churches, it has become almost impossible unless **intentionality** and **tracking** are incorporated into how many individuals are being mentored within a given church.

To illustrate the simplicity of the past, look no further than how many church members were groomed to teach Bible study. Churches would provide Sunday School, church discipleship classes, Sunday morning and evening worship services and Wednesday night Bible study/prayer meeting. Along with these scheduled times to meet, many churches had a mid-week outreach program. Many Bible study teachers were selected from those who showed up to all of these gatherings on a consistent basis. As most involved in the recruitment of church volunteers know, it was hit and miss as to whether they were effective at teaching the Bible.

Today, with the removal of many avenues for church involvement, it is no longer possible to choose Bible study teachers from among the committed who participate in numerous church activities. Also, with the average American moving fourteen times in a lifetime, it is impossible to observe commitment from the longevity of church members' involvement. These obstacles (which might be considered blessings in many ways because of inadequate recruiting) have caused the Church to go in one of two directions. As has already been stated in this book, one direction has been to lower opportunities for church involvement. Another direction has led the church to speed up the process to **identify** potential ministry workers.

Resources that **identify** elements like personality, spiritual gifts, abilities, passion areas and life experiences have greatly enhanced the ability for churches to know their people. Also, databases that have search capabilities have given churches the ability to pinpoint certain individuals for recruitment. While these tools and resources have been effective in **identifying** potential ministry workers, there has been very little either written or discussed as to ways to **multiply** workers.

As has been championed from the beginning of this book, **multiplication** starts with a commitment beyond words and proceeds with a way to measure whether it is actually happening. If you do not know where you are starting, you will not know where you are or how effective you are in the journey to **multiply** workers. Tracking improvement is a major key as to how effective the **multiplication** of God's people for meaningful ministry is at your church. The good news is that with the challenges we face today in **multiplying** God's people, there are plenty of avenues available to meet these challenges.

It's about Relationships, Stupid

Many have attributed Bill Clinton's famous line, "It's the economy, stupid," as being instrumental in electing him President in 1992. When it comes to **multiplying** God's people for mean-ingful ministry, it is not about technology, as great as it may be in assisting God's people to become involved. Nor is it about clever and relevant messages by great communicators, as helpful as they may be in **multiplying** God's people for meaningful ministry. It is also not about all the other cutting-edge concepts and ways to involve people—instead, it is about relationships. The biblical mandate Paul gave Timothy to personally invest in others, who could then invest in still others, has not changed since Paul penned those words in the first century (2 Timothy 2:2).

This chapter has focused on much of my own experiences and for two reasons. First, I have observed and know of so little **multi-plication** taking place in churches across North America. Second-ly, what was taught to me as a new believer has been my practice in ministry for almost 30 years. I have lived in five states since leaving high school and going to college. In all five states, I have taken what was taught me (2 Timothy 2:2) in my early days as a Christian. In whatever I do in ministry, I have attempted to incor-porate 2 Timothy 2:2. My current assignment is to **connect** God's people into meaningful ministry that outlasts them. 2 Timothy 2:2 is as relevant today as when Grady Roan and Don Moye began teaching it to me in 1979. It was not new to them as they took God and His Word as truth.

Conclusion

It was tempting to write just one powerful sentence for this chapter:

---

*Practice the first five commitments—**connecting, identi-fying, equipping, empowering** and **encouraging**—and you will **multiply** God's people for meaningful ministry.*

In a nutshell, this chapter has laid out the first five commitments with an intentional commitment to begin again and again to implement them with God's people, those under the influence of that church and its ministry leaders. The positive results are endless . . .

- a vibrant, reproducing group of believers that will **multiply** their impact long after they have breathed their last breath here on earth

- fellow believers **connecting** in meaningful ministry that will impact long after they have breathed their last breath here on earth

- more of God's people committed to meaningful ministry and more people committed to God's Kingdom

- ...and the story goes on and on. The circle is complete when **multiplying** the first five commitments is practiced.

Figure 8.1

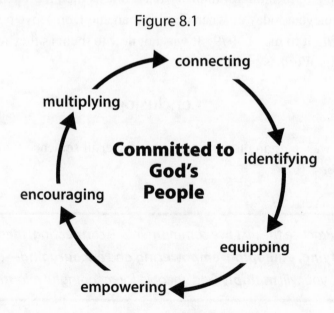

MULTIPLYING Evaluation Survey:
For A CHURCH

O O O

To take the evaluations and score yourself, look on the reverse side of the back jacket of this book. You will find a user ID and password. Go to this website: *http://www.mobilyzr.com/evaluations* and insert your user ID and password. Additional instructions are on the website. Once you are taking the evaluations on the website, the results will be graphed. In this book, you can review the evaluations, but not score yourself or those who take them as a group. Also, there is the opportunity to purchase evaluations and divide them into groups to also assess the effectiveness of various groups within your church or ministry regarding **multiplying** God's people for meaningful ministry.

The evaluations are brief and simple, yet the results can be life-changing for you and your church. Invest just a few minutes of time so you can **identify** where you are and what your next steps need to be in **connecting**, **identifying**, **equipping**, **empowering**, **encouraging** and **multiplying** believers for ministry in YOUR church!

O O O

1. My church provides an intentional process to help potential volunteers discover their competency and passion for ministry before **connecting** in a ministry position.

   Yes ❏   Some Ministries ❏   No ❏   Not Sure ❏

2. My church has an intentional process for those involved in ministry to train new workers for ministry positions.

   Yes ❏   Some Ministries ❏   No ❏   Not Sure ❏

3. My church stresses the importance of those within ministry to apprentice others within the church.

Strongly Agree ❑   Agree ❑   Somewhat Agree/Disagree ❑
Disagree ❑   Strongly Disagree ❑   Not Sure ❑

4. My church has an environment where the senior pastor and/or staff are not expected to fulfill the ministry tasks within the church.

Strongly Agree ❑   Agree ❑   Somewhat Agree/Disagree ❑
Disagree ❑   Strongly Disagree ❑   Not Sure ❑

5. My church believes the senior pastor and staff are primarily called to **equip** the members to carry out the ministry of the church.

Strongly Agree ❑   Agree ❑   Somewhat Agree/Disagree ❑
Disagree ❑   Strongly Disagree ❑   Not Sure ❑

6. My church has a senior pastor who speaks on church members training others to carry out ministry both within and outside the church

Regularly ❑   Often ❑   Sometimes ❑   Rarely ❑
Never ❑   Not Sure ❑

7. My church has an intentional process that pairs a new Christian with a mature Christian to help the new Christian grow in his/her faith.

Yes ❑   Sometimes ❑   No ❑   Not Sure ❑

8. My church holds ministry leaders accountable to reproduce other ministry workers within the church.

Strongly Agree ❑   Agree ❑   Somewhat Agree/Disagree ❑
Disagree ❑   Strongly Disagree ❑   Not Sure ❑

9. My church motivates ministry leaders to invest themselves in potential ministry workers.

Strongly Agree ❑   Agree ❑   Somewhat Agree/Disagree ❑
Disagree ❑   Strongly Disagree ❑   Not Sure ❑

10. My church has a larger percentage of members versus paid staff training members to do and incorporate into ministry.

Yes ❑   No ❑   Not Sure ❑

11. My church is known in the area, or by other churches, as a church that utilizes members to train members for ministry.

Strongly Agree ❑   Agree ❑   Somewhat Agree/Disagree ❑
Disagree ❑   Strongly Disagree ❑   Not Sure ❑

12. My church provides financial resources for lay members to train other lay members in ministry tasks.

Regularly ❑   Often ❑   Sometimes ❑   Rarely ❑
Never ❑   Not Sure ❑

13. My church places a high value on members training other members to fulfill ministry tasks.

Strongly Agree ❑   Agree ❑   Somewhat Agree/Disagree ❑
Disagree ❑   Strongly Disagree ❑   Not Sure ❑

MULTIPLYING Evaluation Survey:
For A MINISTRY

O O O

1. My ministry provides an intentional process to help potential volunteers discover their competency and passion for ministry before **connecting** in a ministry position.

   Yes ❑   Some Ministries ❑   No ❑   Not Sure ❑

2. My ministry has an intentional process for those involved in ministry to train new workers for ministry positions.

   Yes ❑   Some Positions ❑   No ❑   Not Sure ❑

3. My ministry stresses the importance of those within ministry to apprentice others within the ministry.

   Strongly Agree ❑   Agree ❑   Somewhat Agree/Disagree ❑
   Disagree ❑   Strongly Disagree ❑   Not Sure ❑

4. My church has an environment where the senior pastor and/or staff are not expected to fulfill the ministry tasks within the church.

   Strongly Agree ❑   Agree ❑   Somewhat Agree/Disagree ❑
   Disagree ❑   Strongly Disagree ❑   Not Sure ❑

5. My church believes the senior pastor and staff are primarily called to **equip** the members to carry out the ministry of the church.

   Strongly Agree ❑   Agree ❑   Somewhat Agree/Disagree ❑
   Disagree ❑   Strongly Disagree ❑   Not Sure ❑

6. My church has a senior pastor who speaks on church members training others to carry out ministry, both within and outside the church.

Regularly ❑   Often ❑   Sometimes ❑   Rarely ❑
Never ❑   Not Sure ❑

7. My church has an intentional process that pairs a new Christian with a mature Christian to help the new Christian grow in his/her faith.

Yes ❑   Sometimes ❑   No ❑   Not Sure ❑

8. My ministry holds ministry leaders accountable to reproduce other ministry workers within the ministry.

Strongly Agree ❑   Agree ❑   Somewhat Agree/Disagree ❑
Disagree ❑   Strongly Disagree ❑   Not Sure ❑

9. My ministry motivates ministry leaders to invest themselves in potential ministry workers.

Strongly Agree ❑   Agree ❑   Somewhat Agree/Disagree ❑
Disagree ❑   Strongly Disagree ❑   Not Sure ❑

10. My ministry has a larger percentage of lay members versus paid staff training members to do and incorporate into serving within ministry.

Yes ❑   No ❑   Not Sure ❑

11. My ministry is known in the church as a ministry that utilizes members to train other members for ministry.

Strongly Agree ❑   Agree ❑   Somewhat Agree/Disagree ❑
Disagree ❑   Strongly Disagree ❑   Not Sure ❑

12. My ministry provides financial resources for lay members to train other lay members in ministry tasks.

Regularly ❑   Often ❑   Sometimes ❑   Rarely ❑
Never ❑   Not Sure ❑

13. My ministry places a high value on members training other members to fulfill ministry tasks.

Strongly Agree ❑   Agree ❑   Somewhat Agree/Disagree ❑
Disagree ❑   Strongly Disagree ❑   Not Sure ❑

Conclusion

I heard several times by those who previewed this book before it was printed that an entire book could be written on each chapter. I did not disagree, but concluded not many would read a book that consisted of 2000 pages! However, I did throw out the possibility of writing separate books on each chapter that would stand alone, but could also build upon each other.

While I hope God gives me the opportunity to write those books, I conclude this book with a call to commit to **intentionally** incorporating all six elements that have been fleshed out in this book. Without a holistic approach to a commitment to **connect**, **identify**, **equip**, **empower**, **encourage** and **multiply**, the end result will be drastically reduced from what it could be, with all six incorporated holistically into a church.

Carly Fiorina, the former CEO of Hewlett Packard, stated clearer than any person I have read or listened to about the importance of incorporating holistic systems. She said,

> "The required courses for the MS degree included economics, finance, accounting, operations research and organizational behavior . . . I remember Gabe Bitran's course, Management Decision Support

Models, which gave me great insight into the requirement for holistic systems thinking. If only one part or parameter of a complex systems problem is understood or acted upon, the problem cannot be solved. Only by comprehending the whole system—its interactions, dependencies, constraints and pressures—can a real, sustainable improvement be made . . . You've heard the old saying 'to any complex problem, the simple, obvious answer is wrong.' This course proved the point." (2006, p. 82)

While these words by Carly Fiorina are true for business, they are equally as true for a church that commits to **connecting** God's people to meaningful ministry. For years, churches have attempted to **connect** church members to ministry, only to be disappointed with the results. It is time to admit that half-hearted attempts will only create frustration and abandonment in the biblical mandate to **equip** God's people for works of service (Ephesians 4:12).

In an interview with Bill Hybels in *Rev!* magazine, he talks about how "values" must be communicated in a church. He is referring to evangelism when he says,

"...with every value in a church, there's sort of an ebbing and flowing . . . When you stop practicing it, preaching about it, holding it up and challenging people about it, then that value cools off a little bit..." (2006, p. 106)

Whatever the value, the "pastor has to keep bringing it to the consciousness of a congregation. You can't preach on it for a week, every two or three years, and think that the value of evangelism is going to turn white hot." (ibid., 106) If **connecting** God's people to meaningful ministry is to be a value within a church, the same emphasis must be placed on it that Hybels refers to with regard to evangelism.

Over the past year, I have driven into my neighborhood, greeted by a familiar scene almost every day. I pass Cam, a young man who has tied a rope across two trees in his front yard. The distance between the trees is almost exactly the distance between goal posts on a football field. Cam always has 10–12 footballs either beside him or several yards beyond his makeshift goal post. He is committed to becoming a field goal kicker, so day in and day out he kicks field goals through his makeshift goal post. One day, he hopes to kick for a major college football team and beyond college, who knows where he could end up as a kicker.

I have admired his commitment to practice whether the weather is cold or hot. I have admired his commitment to practice kicking without any fanfare as he kicks ball after ball alone in his front yard. I have admired his commitment to forgo short-term pleasures for a long term goal—his dream to be a college kicker. I look forward to following him through his high school career to see if his commitment to kick in college becomes a reality. Whether or not he becomes a college kicker, he will always have one fan (me) that admired him for his commitment to pursue a goal.

If you are reading these words, hopefully you have been committed to read the pages that preceded these words. The financial commitment to purchase this book has been a commitment. My desire is that you will go beyond purchasing and reading the book—that you will make a commitment to incorporate the principles and concepts to **connect** God's people to meaningful ministry as taught in these pages.

I do not know the exact path where this book will take you in your desire to **connect** God's people to meaningful ministry, but I look forward to hearing about your commitment to raise the level of commitment among those God has given you to influence. If I, or the staff I serve with, can serve you in any way to help you strengthen and carry out your commitment to **connect** God's people to meaningful ministry, please don't hesitate to contact us. We are committed to helping you **connect** God's people to meaningful ministry. In advance, thank-you for the privilege to serve you.

Serving Him Together,

Jay McSwain

Bibliography

Beckwith, Harry and Christine Clifford Beckwith. *You, Inc. – The Art of Selling Yourself.* New York, NY: Warner Business Books, 2007

Barna, George. *The Power of Team Leadership.* Colorado Springs, CO: WaterBrook Press, 2001

————. *How To Increase Giving In Your Church.* Ventura, CA: Regal Books, 1997

Chapman, Dr. Gary. *The Five Love Languages.* Chicago, IL: Northfield Publishing, 1992

Dawn, Marva J. *Reaching Out Without Dumbing Down – A Theology of Worship for This Urgent Time.* Grand Rapids, MI: Eerdmans, 1995

Fiorina, Carly. *Tough Choices.* New York, NY: Penguin Group, 2006

Gardner, Howard. "Five Minds For the Future." Boston, MA: Harvard Business School Press, 2006, p. 2

Henderson, Jeff and Andy Stanley. Drive Conference – North Point Ministries, Session 3, 2006

Hybels, Bill. *The Volunteer Revolution.* Grand Rapids, MI: Zondervan, 2004

————. *Rev!* magazine, November/December 2006

Johnson, Lauren Keller. "The New Loyalty: Make It Work for Your Company." *In Harvard Management Update*, May 2005

McArthur, John. *The Truth War*. Nashville, TN: Thomas Nelson Publishers, 2007

McNeal, Reggie. *The Present Future – Six Tough Questions for the CHURCH*. San Francisco, CA: Jossey-Bass, 2003

Peter, Laurence J. *The Peter Principle*. New York, NY: William Morrow & Co., Inc., 1969

Rainer, Thom. *Breakout Churches*. Grand Rapids, MI: Zondervan, 2005

———. *Simple Church*. Nashville, TN: Broadman & Holman Publishers, 2006

Rutz, James H. *The Open Church*. Beaumont, TX: The Seedsowers, 1992

Schaller, Lyle. *The-Seven-Day-A-Week Church*. Nashville, TN: Abingdon Press, 1992

Stanley, Andy. *The Next Generation Leader*. Sisters, OR: Multnomah Publishing, 2003

Vine, W. E. *Expository Dictionary of Old and New Testament Words*. Nashville, TN: Thomas Nelson Publishers, 1996

Warren, Rick. *The Purpose Driven Church*. Grand Rapids, MI: Zondervan, 1995

———. *The Purpose Driven Life*. Grand Rapids, MI: Zondervan, 2002

Witham, Larry A. *Who Shall Lead Them? The Future of Ministry in America*. New York, NY: Oxford University Press, 2005